Citizen's Handbook for Influencing Elected Officials

sunwater
INSTITUTE

Citizen's Handbook for Influencing Elected Officials

Engaging with Congress and State Capitols

Second Edition

BRADFORD FITCH

Hardback ISBN: 979-8-9926897-2-3

Paperback ISBN: 979-8-9926897-3-0

Ebook ISBN: 979-8-9926897-1-6

Cover and interior design: Andy Meaden, meadencreative.com

sunwʌter
INSTITUTE

The Sunwater Institute is a nonpartisan, nonprofit think tank based in North Bethesda, Maryland. Its mission is to strengthen the foundations of liberal democracy through interdisciplinary science, technology, and open dialogue.

The Sunwater Institute believes Congress's performance as an institution is critical to the wellbeing of the nation and democracy worldwide. It conducts theoretical and applied research aimed at improving Congress's institutional knowledge, processes, and efficiency.

The Sunwater Institute strives to convert lessons from its academic research projects into tools, analytics, datasets, publications, and trainings that are leveraged by governments, businesses, academia, media, and nonprofits.

Sunwater.org
Legis1.com

Contents

Acknowledgements 1

About This Book 3

Prologue 5

Introduction 11

PART I HOW GOVERNMENT REALLY WORKS 15

Chapter 1: How Congressional Offices Work 17

1.1.   Dominant Role of Constituents 17

1.2.   Types of Congressional Work 19

1.3.   Offices Are Like Small Businesses 21

1.4.   How Members of Congress Spend Their Time 22

1.5.   What Kind of Mail Do Members of Congress Really Read 24

1.6.   How Congressional Offices Reply to Constituent Mail 26

1.7.   Lawmakers Have More Flexibility to Support You Than You Realize 27

Chapter 2: Congressional Culture 31

2.1.   Working Environment of Congress 31

2.2.   Congressional Hierarchy: Differences Between the House of Representatives and the Senate 33

2.3.   How Power Shifts in Congress Translate to Power Shifts in Constituents 35

2.4.	How Legislative Committees Work	39
2.5.	Congressional Staff Descriptions	43
2.6.	Individual Members of Congress Have More Power Than You Realize	47

Chapter 3: How Lawmakers Make Decisions — 57

3.1.	Heart	58
3.2.	Head	59
3.3.	Health (political)	60

Chapter 4: People Who Can and Can't Influence Legislators and How They Do It — 63

4.1.	Family and Friends Have the Lawmaker's Ear	63
4.2.	Knowledgeable Acquaintances Can Make a Difference	64
4.3.	Legislators Pay Attention to Respected Colleagues	65
4.4.	Legislative Leaders, Arm Twisting, and the Power (or not) of the Party	66
4.5.	The Real Influence of Lobbyists	66
4.6.	What Legislators Want from Lobbyists vs. Constituents	68
4.7.	Campaign Contributors Are Less Influential Than You Think	70
4.8.	Legislators and Polling	71
4.9.	How Paid Advertising Affects Legislators' Thinking	72
4.10.	You Are Competing with Everyone, Even Though You Don't Know It	73

PART II HOW TO INFLUENCE A LEGISLATOR — 75

Chapter 5: Strategies for Influencing Legislators — 77

5.1.	Get to Them BEFORE They Take a Stand	77
5.2.	The Value of a Personal Story	78
5.3.	How to Build Powerful Relationships with Legislators	80
5.4.	Leveraging Your Affiliations to Magnify Your Power	83
5.5.	How to Influence Legislators Who Don't Represent You	87
5.6.	How to Influence Congressional Committee Staff	88
5.7.	Creating a Network and Mobilizing Assets	89
5.8.	How to Map Your Economic and Political Footprint	90
5.9.	How NOT to Advocate	93
5.10.	Building Relationships with Freshman Legislators	94

Chapter 6: Face-to-Face Meetings   99

   6.1.   Scheduling a Meeting with a Legislator   99

   6.2.   Tips for Meeting with Legislators and Staff   102

   6.3.   Tips for Virtual Meetings with Lawmakers and Staff   106

   6.4.   Strategies for In-State Advocacy   108

   6.5.   How to Influence Legislators at Public Meetings   110

   6.6.   Telephone Town Hall Meetings   113

   6.7.   Influencing Staff, and Why It's Important   116

   6.8.   Advocacy During an Election Year   118

   6.9.   Checklist for Preparing and Hosting an Event with an Elected Official   119

Chapter 7: Communications   123

   7.1.   How to Write Letters and Emails to Legislators that Influence Decision-Making   124

   7.2.   Effective (and Ineffective) Phone Calls to Legislators   126

   7.3.   How to Write Letters to the Editor that Get Published   127

   7.4.   Using Social Media to Connect with Lawmakers   129

   7.5.   Engaging Local Media to Support Your Advocacy Efforts   132

   7.6.   Why Petitions Usually Fail to Influence Congress   135

   7.7.   Thank or Spank? After-the-Vote Communications   136

   7.8.   The Magic of Combining Tactics   137

Epilogue   139

Appendix A: Glossary of Congressional Terms   141

Appendix B: Good Books on the U.S. Congress   147

Appendix C: The Advocate's Pledge   151

Appendix D: Legislative Process Flowchart   153

Appendix E: The U.S. Constitution and Amendments   155

Index   173

About the Author   179

About Legis1   180

About The Sunwater Institute   181

Acknowledgements

This edition has been more than a decade in the making and required many individuals to complete. I first thank my publisher, Matt Chervenak of the Sunwater Institute, for suggesting an update to my book, and his wonderful editor, Max Sinsheimer, for his guidance and contributions. Beth McMullen, Suzanne Wronsky, and Laura Cilmi with the Alzheimer's Association were most helpful in outlining their amazing advocacy work. I'm grateful to the dozens of members of Congress and congressional staff who sat through hours of interviews and focus groups. Without their contributions this project would have been impossible to complete.

Finally, I'm grateful to two close "assistants" who worked with me on the final edition: Susanne Fitch and Josephine Fitch. Only through the honest crucible of family critique can a book become a reality.

About This Book

While this book is written by one author, it has many contributors. The author spent 40 years working in and around the United States Congress, interacting with thousands of members of Congress, congressional staff, reporters, lobbyists, and academics. This second edition is more than double the size of the first (which, to be fair, was rather slim). Working for the nonprofit Congressional Management Foundation provided an insider perspective on political decision-making and motivations that only a handful of people are privy to. And as the reader will quickly see, this book draws on insights gathered from focus groups, interviews, news coverage, and research on how legislatures work.

Finally, this text is meant as a practical guide, providing you with tangible concepts and strategies you can implement immediately to become a better citizen-advocate. Even if you don't join a cause, contact a legislator, or write an email to an elected official, this book should provide you with a better understanding of the inner workings of government, offer examples of successful advocacy, and shed light on what really drives politicians in their work.

Prologue

Some years ago, while leading a nonprofit focused on congressional reform, I was recruiting a successful businessman to join our organization. As I explained the value of improving our democratic institutions, he posed an unexpected question to me: "Why does Congress matter?" At first I thought this was an absurd question. Of course Congress matters. It's the premier democratic institution for the most successful nation in the history of our world. But he wanted a more specific answer, and I didn't have it for him. I just assumed that everyone accepted the idea that the U.S. Congress is the most important governmental body in our country.

In recent years, this question of the relevance and resiliency of our democracy has come to the forefront. We've seen survey after survey of Americans having less faith in our democratic institutions, questioning the value of the Constitution, and observing a general rise in authoritarianism in the world. The existential question of why Congress matters is no longer an unusual query. If one is going to make the investment of being a better citizen-advocate, it seems reasonable to ask what the return is on that investment. If our democratic institutions are worthless, if the Congress is so dysfunctional that any level of citizen engagement will fall on deaf ears, why bother?

The answer starts with an appreciation of why Congress matters—not in the abstract, but in terms of how representative government functions. Every society needs a system that attends to the needs and aspirations of the people, while protecting them from internal and external threats. As

James Madison famously said, "If men were angels, no government would be necessary."

In his book *Why Congress*, Philip A. Wallach writes:

> Americans disagree with each other. We have disparate interests, conflicting visions of the good, and divergent judgments about prudent policy. Nevertheless, we must find ways to accommodate each other in addressing the biggest problems of the day, and Congress is the place we must do it. Accordingly, Congress must be a place where many voices find ways to harmonize... When Congress works, its fluctuating coalitions act as engines of national cohesion, and our representatives are able to make regular adjustments to the demands of a changing world.[1]

Put more succinctly in the traditional national motto of the United States: *E pluribus unam*. Translated from Latin, "Out of many, one."

The genius of the Constitution was in giving the nation a system of government that is both master and slave to the People. Unlike the direct democracy of ancient Athens, where every citizen played a role in matters related to the municipality, in a republic the People elect representatives to make the final decision on legislation. Some complain when their elected officials heed their own judgement rather than the majority public opinion of their districts. Yet the Founders did not create a Congress of robotic pollsters, programmed only to follow shifting public opinion. Madison noted the difference between direct democracy (such as Athens) and a republic. "In a democracy, the people meet and exercise the government in person; in a republic, they assemble and administer it by their representatives and agents," he said.

This means any elected official in a democracy must balance varying factors, including their own experience and knowledge. The great English parliamentarian, Edmund Burke, said in 1774 that a true representative must think for themselves. "Your representative owes you, not his industry only,

---

1   *Why Congress,* by Philip A. Wallach (2023).

but his judgement," he said. "And he betrays you instead of serving you if he sacrifices it to your opinion."

On a practical level, the Congress does four things: debates and passes legislation; represents constituents; provides direct governmental services; and conducts oversight of the government and private sector.

Legislates. Most Americans see only this part of the Congress. A C-SPAN view of the House and Senate floor, with the occasional committee hearing. The legislative process moves forth in accordance with the constraints of the Constitution and the rules of each chamber.

Represents Constituents. A fundamental principle in American democracy is the concept of representational government. The great political scientist Richard Fenno, in his seminal book *Home Style: House Members in Their Districts* (1978), described it this way:

> The more accessible they are, House members believe, the more will their constituents be encouraged to feel that they can communicate with the congressman when and if they wish… However, this kind of assurance is not obtained by one-shot offers. It is created over a long time and underwritten by trust. Access and the assurance of access, communication and the assurance of communication—these are the irreducible underpinnings of representation.

Nearly every member of Congress believes that it is their moral and political responsibility to seek and identify the needs and aspirations of their constituents.

Provides Services for Constituents. Most people are unaware that every congressional office has a customer service operation within. These workers, called field representatives or case workers, can respond to and assist with a variety of constituent requests—everything from resolving an immigration problem to navigating the loan application process at the Small Business Administration. Sometimes Congress is the "last line" of support for a desperate citizen. In 2020, at the start of the pandemic, a despondent mom, eight-months pregnant with her second child, could not find a necessity in short supply at the time: toilet paper. In a last-ditch effort, she called her congresswoman. When the mom got home from the hospital with her new baby, she found a carton of toilet paper on her front porch. This simple act of public service and kindness went well beyond the tangible act involving toilet paper. In her thank-you note to the congresswoman she wrote emphatically, "Thank you for SEEING me!"

Conducting Oversight. One of the important components of our checks-and-balances system is the ability of Congress to exercise oversight of the executive branch. Sometimes these can be quite weighty topics, such as the Iran-Contra hearings or the Select Committee to Investigate the January 6th Attack on the U.S. Capitol. This role can extend to private sector investigations as well. Years ago, Wells Fargo Bank was at the receiving end of a bipartisan drumming at a congressional hearing for various misdeeds. (It seemed that the only thing Democrats and Republicans could agree on was that beating up bankers on TV was good politics.) Sometimes these hearings and investigations can devolve into public spectacle. But they can also form the groundwork for genuine government reform or societal improvement. The great congressman from Indiana, Lee Hamilton, put it this way. "Part of Congress's job is to monitor and oversee the executive branch. There is no question that this role can be used to pursue partisan ends, but it can also be used to ensure that agencies and officials are actually serving Americans as they should. It helps ordinary Americans peer into the workings of government."

When considering the question "Why does Congress matter?" it helps to look at the historical evidence. Some of the most important advancements as a nation—and the greatest benefits extended to the American people—have come through acts of Congress. Take the Homestead Act of 1862, signed into law by President Abraham Lincoln. Its impact was enormous: more than 160 million acres (250,000 square miles of public land, or nearly 10 percent of the total area of the United States) were given away free of charge to 1.6 million homesteaders. In the early 1900s, child labor laws saved millions of children from horrible working conditions. In the 1960s, Congress created Social Security, Medicare, and Medicaid, lifting millions of Americans out of poverty. Civil rights and voting rights laws transformed the relationship between Black Americans and their government. And in 2021, Congress passed a bipartisan infrastructure bill that will invest $1 trillion to improve roads, bridges, internet services, and much more.

Perhaps the best answer to why Congress matters comes from the great documentary producer, Ken Burns. One of his earlier works was *The Congress* (1988), a rich and thorough examination of the first branch of government. Early in the documentary, narrator David McCullough eloquently recites the impact of Congress on the nation and the world.

> In 200 years, Congress has in the name of the People pushed open the West, built railroads, freed slaves, made war, passed Social Security, put G.I.s through college, and paid to land men on the moon. They've driven Indians from their land, outlawed alcohol, and filibustered without mercy. They created Mother's Day and daylight savings time. Dominated presidents and been dominated by them. Started wars and stopped them. "Congress," Thomas Jefferson said, "is the great commanding theater of this nation. It is the place where laws are made."

Assuming the reader is sufficiently persuaded that Congress and state legislatures are relevant and worthy of our attention, let us now turn to the question of how average citizens can influence them.

Introduction

"We do not have a government of the majority—we have a government of the majority who participate." That statement by Thomas Jefferson reminds us that legislative outcomes in a democracy are not random events. It affirms the belief that if citizens participate in the democratic process, their voices can make a difference. And it promotes the noble democratic ideals and structures established by the Founders, and the proposition that our voice can improve the human condition.

But over the decades Americans have come to believe their voices do not make a difference. Tales of influence-peddling, media stories focusing on corruption, and movies and TV shows that portray Congress as selfish and dishonest have reinforced the notion that "special interests" control Washington. Scandals involving unethical legislators trading favors with trips, gifts, and meals reinforce the idea that the average citizen is powerless against well-heeled lobbyists. We are told it's a waste of time to write an email, make a phone call, or attend a town hall meeting. Members of Congress themselves on the campaign trail perpetuate the notion that Washington is corrupt: "Just elect *me* and I'll fix the problem." The real agenda is set in a smoky backroom by special interest fat-cats and self-interested legislators, and the citizen's opinion isn't worth the time it takes to make a phone call to a congressman's office.

Here's the truth: they're wrong and Thomas Jefferson was right. Citizens who participate in the democratic process are overwhelmingly the most influential component in any lawmaker's decision-making. Lunches with lobbyists may occur every day in Washington, and narrow interests occasionally succeed at achieving legislative goals that do not seem to be in the public interest. However, *most* of the factors that make up the congressional agenda, *most* of the legislation that is eventually passed by Congress, and nearly *all* individual decisions made by members of Congress are directly influenced by citizens who participate. People writing letters, sending emails, attending town hall meetings, visiting lawmakers—they are the dominant influence on legislative outcomes.

This idea may challenge popular belief, but this book will show—through surveys of staff, individual interviews with legislators and staff, and analysis of real decision-making—that citizens drive legislative outcomes. While researching this book the author was given unprecedented access to legislators and staff who offered candid, off-the-record insights into legislative decision-making. What emerged is a portrait of the process that stands in stark contrast to its portrayal in popular media.

The key to this conclusion is not found in front-page headlines, but in the day-to-day drudgery of congressional work. What most Americans and journalists see is only a fraction of the work and decisions Congress engages in. Journalistic legend Edward R. Murrow described the media as a "searching spotlight" focusing on a tiny, interesting object for a brief moment, only to move away moments later. The perception may be that Congress is influenced by "special interests," but that perception is based mostly on what the searching spotlight focuses upon. Few reporters or researchers have been given the access to legislators and congressional staff, or take the time, to view the *totality* of legislators' decision-making processes.

Very few decisions legislators make—whether to vote for or against legislation, to cosponsor a bill, or to offer an amendment at a committee hearing—garner a whit of attention, except perhaps to a small group of constituents in the legislator's state or district. Most of the questions legislators face are *not* the major issues of the day. "A lot of things that constituents come to us with are not from the daily headlines," said one House chief of staff. Members of Congress and staff struggle with hundreds of issues each week that do not affect life-and-death, war-and-peace issues. Should Congress impose a ban on transporting horses in double-decker trailers? Should funding for hospice care for the elderly be increased, and if so, what should be cut to pay for it? Should the ethanol blend levels in gasoline be increased from 10 percent to 15 percent? Such questions are typical of a legislator's workday.

While the news media show a Washington where men and women struggle with complex problems—and indeed they do—what you don't see are the less titanic questions that make up most of the work of Congress. These issues are of particular interest to groups of citizens because they affect their livelihood or represent a cause they believe in. And most of the lobbying dollars, constituent visits, and legislative haggling revolve around these kinds of issues that rarely make it into your local newspaper or onto a national TV news show.

Nonetheless, getting involved politically is intimidating. It's hard to stand up at a town hall meeting in front of your neighbors and tell a member of Congress or a state legislator what you think. This book offers practical guidance on how to prepare for meetings with legislators, write effective letters and emails, craft letters to the editor that catch lawmakers' attention, and understand the most effective ways to influence legislative staff.

Once you recognize that most legislative decisions never make the front page, yet still profoundly impact your life; once you see that those decisions are not influenced by lobbyists and "special interests," but by regular citizens; once you master the basic—but crucial—skills to influence undecided lawmakers, you will be ready to *participate* in the most important conversation humankind ever conceived: the democratic dialogue. This book will show you how.

PART I
HOW GOVERNMENT REALLY WORKS

In any attempt to influence a group of people it is important to understand their environment. The congressional and state legislative environments are different than other workplaces, and those who appreciate their special characteristics are most successful at achieving their advocacy goals.

Citizen-advocates frequently make the mistake of looking at legislatures through the prism of their own work environment: business owners envision Congress as a business, teachers think it must be like a school, and doctors think it works like a hospital. It is natural to draw from personal work experience, but it is sometimes detrimental to your cause. It is true that Capitol Hill often resembles a group of independently operating small businesses, the hierarchical nature of the institution feels like a high school, and the rush of activity mirrors that of an emergency room. Yet the overall environment and the way things get done are unique in our nation. Understanding that environment is vital to winning in the legislative process.

Chapter 1
How Congressional Offices Work

You campaign in poetry; you govern in prose.
— **Gov. Mario Cuomo**

1.1. Dominant Role of Constituents

Constituents drive nearly all decision-making in congressional offices. (See Chart 3 in Chapter 5 for details on what influences members of Congress.) "I prioritize everything based on anything that's connected to constituents," said one Republican lawmaker. "I want feedback from the real world."

Our system is set up in such a way that legislators are beholden first and foremost to the people they represent. The House and Senate rules reinforce this connection by legally prohibiting members of Congress from spending office money on behalf of non-constituents. (This has put a crimp in the plans of a few House members who wanted to spend taxpayer money to travel outside their congressional district in a Senate or gubernatorial race.)

There are two types of constituents who interact with legislators: those with an *interest* and those with an *opinion*. If a woman stands up at a town hall meeting and says, "I think we should get our troops out of Afghanistan," the congresswoman will file that in one part of her brain. But if a different woman says, "I think we should get our troops out of Afghanistan because my son is stationed there," the congresswoman files it into a completely different compartment. The second woman has a stronger bond to the legislator, and she has a much greater obligation to integrate the woman's concerns into her decision-making. Ironically, advocates tend to be more passionate about those issues in which they don't have an interest, but about which they feel strongly. You see much more emotion in emails to Congress from People for the Ethical Treatment of Animals (PETA) about the treatment of baby seals than you do from American Medical Association (AMA) members concerned about Medicare reimbursement rates.

Traditionally, members of Congress rarely accept meetings with non-constituents or answer mail from outside their district or state. This might frustrate groups who want to influence someone who does not have a constituent connection to their organization, but their beef is with the Founders who designed our system of government. If you want to influence a member of Congress who does not represent you, the best course of action is to get *your* legislator to influence them. If she won't do it, then vote her out of office. (There are some methods for influencing legislators who don't represent you, and they are reviewed in Section 5.5.)

When setting a legislator's daily agenda, constituents always figure prominently. Any constituent who makes the effort to travel to Washington will almost always get a meeting with a member of Congress or his staff. One freshman lawmaker from the West Coast established a personal policy of meeting with *every* constituent who traveled to Washington—but had to abandon the policy after a few months because he was shirking his legislative duties.

Every constituent who writes their own letter or email to Congress will almost surely get some kind of response, and their message will be integrated into the decision-making process in some way. Meetings in the district or state, town hall meetings, and chance encounters on the street are all incredibly influential to legislators, as they know that their very employment is dependent upon understanding their constituents' views. One Republican Senator said, "I have told paid lobbyists for years that any lobbyist worth his salt will concentrate on getting my constituents to tell me what they think… not what he thinks. He better spend his time getting them to write me because that's who I listen to." Indeed, members of Congress are experts at gauging public opinion and are the best pollsters of their constituents—as they're the only pollsters who lose their jobs if they get the answer wrong. One House chief of staff noted this about constituents: "In some ways they don't understand the depth of their power."

1.2. Types of Congressional Work

Congressional offices are divided into three types: *personal* offices (serving the individual members of Congress), *committee* offices, and *leadership* offices. Most of the lobbying that advocacy groups engage in is directed to legislators' personal offices. The organization of congressional personal offices has evolved over Congress's history. The modern system came into existence in the 1970s and has not changed much since then. Offices have two responsibilities: *legislative* and *representational.* These responsibilities are divided between two types of offices: the Washington office (legislative) and the district or state office (representational).

The legislative work is what most people read about: writing laws, sitting in committee hearings, and voting on bills. Members and their staff debate the issues of the day and try to develop solutions to societal problems, all playing out on the grand stages of the House and Senate. While the legislative work gets the most attention, it accounts for less than half of the labor undertaken by a personal office.

Representational Work

Most of a congressional office's resources and personnel are dedicated to representational duties. This work mostly is in response to individual constituent questions and requests, and centers on two functions: casework and answering constituent mail (which is now all email).

"Casework" is the term used in Congress to describe individual requests from constituents for the legislator to intervene on their behalf with a government agency. These requests range from helping a senior citizen recover a lost Social Security check, to aiding a disabled worker in obtaining worker's compensation. By far the dominant casework request relates to immigration issues. Even in offices located far from the southern border, immigration-related casework requests can make up one-third of a congressional district office's workload. Requests for last-minute passports, green cards to avoid deportation, and educational visas are common.

A member of Congress's Washington office also spends a great deal of time on another representational duty: answering mail. "Mail" includes any kind of constituent communication—letter, fax, postcard, petition, phone call, or email. In 2001, anthrax-laced letters were sent to several congressional offices, resulting in five postal workers' deaths. As a result, Congress moved all paper mail sorting to a secure off-site location. Now all paper mail sent to Congress is digitally scanned and sent electronically to individual office databases. Staff sort and process these opinions, pleas, and criticisms as best they can. Overall, Congress receives about 50 million emails a year, with some House offices receiving more than 180,000 annually.

In most House offices, one junior staffer sorts the mail and drafts responses to some of it. The rest is doled out to two or three legislative assistants. The draft responses are usually reviewed by a legislative director and chief of staff. Any new language that articulates a policy position is typically reviewed personally by the member of Congress. In the Senate, more staff are involved, but the workflow is similar. Legislators are often given summary reports that indicate which issues or positions are getting the most mail.

Because of the constant flood of communications into congressional offices, it is vital that constituents add their own voice to their message. Unedited form communications sent en masse by organizations hold little sway. Yet a well-written, personalized email will surely at least be read by a staff member—or even by a legislator themselves. (For more on what kind of mail legislators really read, see Section 1.5.)

Legislative Work

On the legislative side, member personal offices are little research factories. They collect information, distill relevant data, and produce outputs in the form of memos, bills, letters, and press releases. Staff attend hearings, draft statements, summarize reports, and produce memos for the legislator. When approaching a decision, the legislator will always consult his staff expert on the topic and usually follow their recommendations. This does not mean that staff control all decision-making; they do not. Rather, it means that staff are usually in tune with their boss's thinking, and guide them to a decision they assume the legislator desires.

Legislative staff serve as both research assistants and policy advisors to members of Congress. They investigate the facts of an issue, gather the positions of interested parties, analyze the implications for constituents, and synthesize the information for legislators. Legislative assistants (known as LAs) also offer policy recommendations on almost every issue in their portfolio. They become policy experts, no matter how limited their experience with the issue, and pride themselves on their ability to influence legislators.

1.3. Offices Are Like Small Businesses

Legislator offices are not alike. In fact, Congress is actually an amalgamation of 541[2] small businesses, not a monolithic institution. Each office has the same burdens and challenges of a small business: each is given a budget and required to hire staff, purchase equipment and furniture, find office space, and provide services to customers (constituents). But because they operate within the federal government, the managers of these businesses (the members of Congress, chiefs of staff, and office managers) must also navigate the layers of red tape typical of a bureaucracy. For example, while

....
2   Congress is made up of 100 senators, 435 representatives, and 6 non-voting delegates. Delegates may not be able to vote on the House floor but exercise full rights in committees—often making them more powerful that junior House members with floor privileges.

they are responsible for buying their own computers, they must also comply with various regulations and fill out various forms just to complete the purchase.

Each office is given an annual budget. House offices are allocated about $1.5 million; Senate budgets are larger and vary depending upon the size of the state. Most of this money goes to staff salaries. House offices are limited to 18 full-time and four part-time staff; Senate offices vary, employing anywhere from 25 to 100 staffers. Both chambers are supported by institutional offices and staffs who assist individual member offices with logistics like phone installation, I.T. and software needs, furniture, and more.

This "independent" office system leads to varying degrees of efficiencies and effectiveness. For example, one senior House member has repeatedly overspent his office budget. House office budget rules—which wisely incentivize thriftiness—forced him to personally reimburse the government for the overage. And yet, this same member chaired an important committee.

For the citizen-advocate, the corresponding variance in "customer service" can be quite relevant. If a legislator is not adept at answering his email or integrating it into his decision-making process, then in-person meetings and raising questions at town hall events will be more influential. But if a legislator has a solid system for analyzing public opinion based on constituent email, launching a targeted and personalized email campaign with an action alert could produce the desired effect.

1.4. How Members of Congress Spend Their Time

Members of Congress work on average 70 hours a week when Congress is in session and about 60 hours a week when home during recesses.[3] (Before the reader makes a joke about their productivity, this reflects their work *ethic* not their work *product*.) Their day in Washington usually runs from 8:00

---

3   Congressional Management Foundation and Society for Human Resource Management, "Life in Congress: The Member Perspective" (2013).

a.m. to after 9:00 p.m. Below is a composite sample schedule of a member of Congress. You'll notice that in some cases the lawmaker is double-booked, a common practice due to the demands on their time.

8:00 a.m. – 9:00 a.m.	Attend Fundraiser for State Delegation Colleague at National Party HQ
9:00 a.m. – 9:15 a.m.	Personal Staff Meeting at Office
9:30 a.m. – 11:30 a.m.	Hearing. House Judiciary Subcommittee on Courts, Intellectual Property, and the Internet. Topic: Intellectual Property Litigation and the U.S. International Trade Commission
10:00 a.m. – 12:00 p.m.	Hearing. House Committee on Agriculture. Topic: Food Distribution Program on Indian Reservations (FDPIR)
12:00 p.m. – 1:00 p.m.	Party Caucus Meeting
1:00 p.m. – 1:20 p.m.	Meeting. Emergency Nurses Association. Topic: Workplace/Emergency Room Violence Protection Act
1:20 p.m. – 1:45 p.m.	Meeting: American Society of Civil Engineers. Topic: Grants to Local Communities through Infrastructure Investment and Jobs Act
2:00 p.m. – 3:00 p.m.	Fundraising Call Time at National Party HQ
2:30 p.m. – 3:30 p.m.	Briefing: Central Intelligence Agency Briefing on International Terrorist Threats Against Americans Living in Europe
3:30 p.m. – 4:00 p.m.	Meeting. Local County Executives from the District. Topic: Broadband Equity Access and Deployment (BEAD) Program
4:00 p.m. – 4:30 p.m.	Meeting. Rep. Joe Smith, Dean of State House Delegation. Topic: Strategy for Lobbying Party Steering and Policy Committee to be Accepted on House Appropriations Committee Next Year
4:30 p.m. – 4:45 p.m.	Interview. Local TV Station via Satellite. Topic: Expanding Internet Broadband in the District.
4:45 p.m. – 5:00 p.m.	Meeting (Internal). Office Scheduler to Review Tomorrow's Schedule.
5:00 p.m. – 6:00 p.m.	Meeting. Women's Caucus. Topic: Developing/Discussing Priorities for the Remainder of the Year

6:00 p.m. – 7:30 p.m.	Attend Various Fundraisers for Committee Colleagues
7:30 p.m. – 9:00 p.m.	Lead Telephone Town Hall Meeting with Constituents

1.5. What Kind of Mail Do Members of Congress Really Read

There is an extraordinary cynicism in America about the degree to which legislators listen to their constituents. This often shows up in the belief that messages sent to legislators are not really integrated into policy decision-making, and that, if the messages are read at all, it's only by staff or interns.

This belief is mostly inaccurate. Individualized communications that include some expression of personal sentiment or opinion are the most likely to be influential. The importance of constituent mail was best expressed by a Senate chief of staff who participated in a focus group in November 2001— two months after the 9/11 terrorist attacks on New York and Washington, and one month after an anthrax attack had completely shut down the delivery of paper mail to the U.S. Congress. He noted that his boss, the senator, felt cut off. "He feels like he doesn't know what's going on," the chief of staff said. "He really misses the mail."

Nearly all legislators use constituent communications as a gauge of public opinion. One House chief of staff put it this way: "Sometimes constituent mail is the canary in the coal mine. If we get ten or fifteen people writing in spontaneously it's going to get our attention," she said. But not all letters, postcards, or emails reach the desk of a member of Congress. Staff identify communications which in some way help the legislator understand constituents' feelings, validate or contest the legislator's opinion, or just make her feel good.

These are the types and characteristics of communications most likely to be identified by staff and presented to legislators as representative of public opinion.

Well-Written

A carefully crafted message still carries weight. The value and power of the written word has not changed since the time of *The Odyssey*.

Passionate

Messages that convey genuine feeling are most likely to be read by decision-makers. Everyone wishes to be moved by words, even members of Congress. It's best to paint a picture for the legislator and their staff. Describe in vivid detail how an issue affects you and your community.

Funny

Think about the emails you forward to friends. Then think about how you can convey that feeling in a communication to a legislator, while still making your point.

Written by Children

The younger generation holds a special place in the policymaking process. Communications from kids get extra attention in nearly every legislator's office, as public officials feel it is part of their responsibility to teach the next generation about the role of government and democracy in society.

Representative of a Group

Staff will sometimes identify communications that may not be well written or passionate but clearly express a view shared by many in the district. They look for both quantitative and qualitative data to help legislators make decisions, and sometimes an email that just articulates the "average Joe's" opinion clarifies the opinions of thousands more. A few years ago, Congress was considering a bill which would overturn an EPA regulation affecting dry cleaners. The regulation was intended to improve the environment by using better chemicals in the cleaning process. However, they were more expensive to use. One dry cleaner wrote his member of Congress explaining his predicament and said, "If this regulation stands, I'm going to have to lay off one of my employees." That email went to the top of the "to-read" pile.

Thank You Notes

A guaranteed way of seeing that your email gets printed and put on the desk of a member of Congress is to say, "thank you." Very few groups or individuals thank legislators for the work they do, so those who do get their messages passed on. It's not just a polite thing to do—it likely will be remembered the next time the legislator is visited by the constituent or the lobbyist who represents them.

1.6. How Congressional Offices Reply to Constituent Mail

Congress gets about 50 million emails a year from constituents, so a big part of the labor investment in a congressional office is responding to those communications. In the late 1990s private companies started selling customized software to trade associations and nonprofits to facilitate emails to Capitol Hill. If you belong to a group, you may have received an "Action Alert" with a pre-populated text to send to your state or federal lawmakers. Working jointly with the House and Senate, these software companies have synced the delivery of the messages to ensure that only constituents can communicate with their elected officials. So, if you use one of the systems, you can be assured your message will be delivered.

How a congressional office responds to those messages varies widely. Every House and Senate office operates a little differently. Some have outstanding constituent mail operations and respond to citizen emails and letters within a few days. Others are poorly managed, and it might take months to get a reply. Generally, they all follow the same process.

Step 1: Every message is scanned by a staffer to determine relevancy and to prepare to respond. The communication arrives in the office and is logged by an intern or data entry staff, categorized, and assigned to a staff member to draft a reply.

Step 2: Identical form communications are separated from individualized ones. These are scanned to determine if the legislator has already approved a standard reply to the constituent's question or plea. If existing text is available, a reply is immediately prepared and sent. Nearly all offices prepare reports summarizing the form communications received and provide them to senior staff and the member of Congress to gauge public opinion on the issue.

Step 3: If the legislator has never answered the question or issue posed by the constituent, a staff member will draft a reply.

Step 4: Draft replies to new or complex issues are usually reviewed by a senior staffer, such as the legislative director or chief of staff.

Step 5: Members of Congress vary in their practices of reading and approving constituent correspondence. Some legislators read *every* letter and email. Some go through multiple drafts for replies, delaying the response time by weeks or even months. The best managed offices give staff wide latitude to use their judgment as to what the member of Congress needs to see. She'll only get draft replies that articulate a new position, discuss a controversial issue, or are being sent to key stakeholders in the district or state. Staff will use other source material—speeches, website content, and hearing testimony—to craft replies to constituents that capture the essence of the legislator's opinion.

1.7. Lawmakers Have More Flexibility to Support You Than You Realize

Most people assume that state and federal lawmakers are more robot than human, simply following the orders of party leadership, special interest groups, or their campaign contributors. In fact, legislators have significant flexibility in responding to, adhering to, or opposing a constituent's request. This unexpected latitude is due to the reality that *most* of the requests lawmakers consider neither affect their re-election nor have a lasting impact on their public reputation.

There are, however, a few issues that do have either *electoral* or *reputational* impact. For the past few decades these usually include abortion, guns, immigration, and (sometimes) healthcare. For example, in 2010, Republicans used negative feelings about the Affordable Care Act ("Obamacare") to gain a majority in the House. In 2018, Democrats then used the growing popularity of that same law to win back the House.

When one examines all the bills and votes that a member of Congress considers, a tiny fraction is genuinely controversial. Most requests for support or opposition affect only a particular profession (represented by a trade association), a nonprofit's mission (backed by donors and supporters), or a company. Parkinson's disease patients and their families want increased funding to find a cure to this tragic disease; ophthalmologists are opposed to allowing optometrists access to laser technology to help patients at Veterans Affairs hospitals; animal rights activists lobby against the transportation of horses on double-decker buses. Unless you subscribe to the legislative newsletters of any of these groups, you're unlikely to know that these issues exist. And while Parkinson's patients, ophthalmologists, and animal rights activists would like to believe that elections are won and lost on their issues, that just isn't the political reality we live in.

For citizen-advocates, this is great news. If a constituent can demonstrate the impact of a bill or issue on their family, community, or state, lawmakers have the freedom to act without facing any negative political consequences.

During the debate over the Affordable Care Act, one medical professional group opposed a pending amendment that would have negatively affected them and possibly inconvenienced constituents. One member of this group described her interaction with a lawmaker this way: "I told him, 'Congressman, if you vote for this amendment and it passes, your constituents will have to drive farther and pay more money for the same procedure they get today,'" she said. "The congressman turned to his aide and said, 'we're done—what's next?'" It isn't campaign contributions, congressional leadership, or mysterious special interests that influence most lawmakers' decisions; it's constituents making clear that their district or state will be directly affected—positively or negatively—depending on how the lawmaker responds.

Chapter 2
Congressional Culture

Serving in Congress is like having a second shot at high school.

— Rep. Barney Frank (D-Massachusetts)

Jack McIver Weatherford's book *Tribes on the Hill* divided Congress up in anthropological terms, which is an apt way of looking at its culture and environment. Congress is a balance of tribes: the youthful staff toiling in offices, the optimistic freshman members who believe *their* generation will be the one to push aside partisan disagreement, the cynical reporters pouncing on any minor misstep and spotlighting any flaw, and the crusty old lion senators who fill the chamber with grand rhetoric. This mix results in a strange and dynamic clash of old and new, fury and calm, breeding a conflicting system that suggests that anything is possible, but that little can be accomplished.

2.1. Working Environment of Congress

The work schedule is brutal. Sixty-hour weeks are common—seventy or eighty hours is the norm in the final days leading up to a congressional recess. Congressional leaders for years have sought to replace the phrase

"Congressional Recess" with "District Work Period," as "recess" conjures up images of legislators frolicking about, playing kickball and goofing off. In fact, when members of Congress are home their schedules are packed with 10-hour days of constituent meetings, public events, speeches, and other district-oriented activities.

The working environment for congressional staff is not how it is portrayed in Hollywood. The pace is fast, but the work can be mundane, and the offices are cramped. Basic labor laws didn't even apply to congressional employees until 1995, when Congress passed the Congressional Accountability Act. Since then, Congress has been required to comply with a series of worker protection laws, such as the Civil Rights Act and the Fair Labor Standards Act. Before these reforms, Congress was exempt from most labor laws that the rest of the country had to adhere to.[4] Congress had such a poor reputation for working conditions it was often referred to in the 1980s as "The Last Plantation."

Quarters are so cramped that offices sometimes create workspaces in rooms designed for storage. If you walk up to the fifth floor of the Cannon House Office Building, don't be surprised if you see interns working in what appear to be storage cages. While this practice has fallen out of favor in recent years, the pressure to produce reams of work has not abated. Congress feels it cannot add more staff or create new office buildings for fear of being accused of spending money on itself. As a result, the number of staff that a House member is allotted by law has not changed since 1979, even though the workload has grown exponentially.

Happily, there have been some improvements to the work environment in recent years. In part due to pressure from outside groups, Congress began paying its interns in 2018. This is not just an altruistic development. Internships are the easiest path to employment on Capitol Hill. If internships were restricted to only those college students who could afford to live in Washington, D.C., for three months, then only wealthier students would

---

4   The reason Congress exempted itself from these laws was not political, it was constitutional. Because the Constitution requires a separation of powers between the legislative branch and executive branch, most legal scholars opined that it was unconstitutional for the executive branch to enforce labor requirements/standards on the legislative branch.

be viable candidates for full-time jobs. Due in part to recommendations of the Select Committee on the Modernization of Congress, House office budgets received about a 20 percent increase in 2020, restoring cuts which started in 2011. Still, it has become increasingly difficult for Congress to retain talented staff, putting the legislative branch at a disadvantage in its competition with the executive branch and the private sector.

2.2. Congressional Hierarchy: Differences Between the House of Representatives and the Senate

There are significant differences between members of the House of Representatives and the Senate.

The U.S. House of Representatives

Members of the House of Representatives serve a two-year term. This means they are held accountable by their constituents relatively quickly. For example, if a state has a primary election in March, a freshman House member may face their first test at the ballot box just 14 months after being sworn into office. Unlike the Senate, the House is very hierarchical, almost like high school, with freshman legislators seeking to make an impression, aggressive subcommittee chairmen looking for angles to reach leadership levels, and senior members ruling on the most important matters.

Each House member is looking for their own niche issue: a legislative topic where they can become an expert, introduce bills, and serve as the go-to source for reporters. Members who rise to leadership positions generally set the agenda and often determine the fate of legislation on the House floor. Committee and subcommittee chairs are like gatekeepers, determining which bills to consider, hearings to hold, and topics to prioritize for oversight of the executive branch or the private sector.

Unless they represent a state with a single House seat, most House members serve districts of about 750,000 people, with a decennial census guiding a redistricting process to shape the lines and rebalance the population. Most legislative work in the House happens in committees, with members wrangling with colleagues and committee chairs to get their amendments adopted. Many, but not all, outcomes are determined along party lines.

For a bill to come to the House floor, unless an expedited procedure is authorized by House leadership, it must have an accompanying rule. This rule is determined by the House Rules Committee, which is usually controlled by the Speaker of the House.[5] Members petition the House Rules Committee to grant their amendment a vote on the House floor, usually in a hearing held in the U.S. Capitol building. Most are denied, so getting a vote on a member's amendment is one of the clearest signs the legislator has the respect of their colleagues.

The U.S. Senate

Senators are elected to six-year terms. They enjoy significantly more independence than their House counterparts—and more power. The Senate is often called "the world's most exclusive club." Unlike the House, the Senate is not guided by a specific set of rules, but rather through consensus. It usually requires "unanimous consent" for any legislation to be considered, so any one senator can derail the entire agenda. Even the Senate Majority Leader, who is the most powerful member of the institution, recognizes that a single senator can derail any legislative initiative. For example, in 2024, Senator Tommy Tuberville (R-Alabama) blocked the nomination of hundreds of the Department of Defense officer nominations because he objected to certain policies adopted by the Pentagon.

You will often hear media pundits claim the Democrats or Republicans "control" the Senate. Know this: no one "controls" the Senate. Under traditional practice, senators can offer unlimited amendments and have no limitations on how long they can speak on the Senate floor. Because of

---

5   In the 118th Congress (2023–2024), to gain enough votes to be elected Speaker of the House, Rep. Kevin McCarthy (R-California) made the unprecedented decision to appoint three Republicans to the House Rules Committee who generally didn't follow his leadership or direction. As a result, under Speaker McCarthy, and then under Speaker Mike Johnson, the Speaker did not have complete control of the rules which guided legislation on the House floor.

this latter tradition, senators can block legislation by declaring a "filibuster," which requires 60 votes to overcome before bringing legislation for a vote. Allowing the Senate to take its time reviewing pending legislation to ensure it would benefit the nation was the Founders' way of balancing the hot and sudden passions of the House. George Washington is said to have told Thomas Jefferson that the framers created the Senate to "cool" House legislation, just as a saucer is used to cool hot tea.

A debate arose in recent years as to whether the Senate should abolish the filibuster and be guided by simple majority. While this would make the Senate more like the House (and Congress more like a European parliament), it would also mean that major legislation would not require bipartisan support to pass. Because of this rule and practice, senators are more inclined to work in small bipartisan groups (sometimes called "gangs") to develop legislative compromises. In 2009 a "Gang of Six" senators worked on debt reform. The massive bipartisan infrastructure bill passed in 2021[6] and the proposed immigration legislation of 2024 both emanated from a small bipartisan group of senators hammering out deals. The inspiration for compromise usually starts with two senators—a Democrat and Republican—expressing a desire to achieve a public policy goal and a willingness to compromise on certain issues to achieve that goal.

2.3. How Power Shifts in Congress Translate to Power Shifts in Constituents

On April 10, 2024, Larry Heikkila, the Mayor of Norman, Oklahoma, became more powerful than he had been the day before. It was nothing that Mayor Heikkila did; rather, his friend, Rep. Tom Cole (R-Oklahoma), who represents that part of Oklahoma, ascended to the chair of the powerful House Appropriations Committee after Rep. Kay Granger (R-Texas) resigned from the position.

---

6   The nucleus of the "gang" that wrote the infrastructure bill was Senate Democrat Kyrsten Sinema and Senate Republican Rob Portman. They had bonded years earlier on a congressional delegation trip to Selma, Alabama. Congressional travel is a common way for legislators to become friends, which often leads to valuable legislation benefiting the nation.

The chair of the House Appropriations Committee is arguably the third most powerful person in Washington, surpassed only by the Speaker of the House and the President. One might ask, isn't the Senate Majority Leader more powerful? Under Senate rules and tradition, the Senate Majority Leader needs the approval of 99 Senate colleagues if he wants to name a post office. In contrast, the chair of the House Appropriations Committee has significant sway over $1.7 trillion in annual discretionary funding—everything except the military, and guaranteed benefit programs such as Social Security.

That means if Mayor Heikkila wants a road widened or a bridge repaired or new awnings for Main Street businesses, he just puts in a request with his new best friend, Tom Cole. And starting in 2021, the House Appropriations Committee brought back the so-called "earmark" system, where members of Congress can make requests for projects to be funded in their districts. This meant members of Congress could once again direct federal dollars toward small, local projects.

The purpose of the above illustration is to demonstrate that not all constituents are alike—those represented by more powerful lawmakers can have greater influence over public policy *because* they have the ear of that powerful lawmaker. When majorities shift in either congressional chamber, it's not just a shuffling of power amongst the power brokers; a similar power transfer is happening in communities throughout the nation. So, in 2013 when Senator Max Baucus (D-Montana) resigned his seat as chair of the Senate Finance Committee, passing the gavel to Senator Ron Wyden (R-Oregon), every bank, corporation, nonprofit, and trade association in Oregon took notice—searching their internal databases for members or employees from Oregon who might know someone on the new chairman's staff.

Constituents are often shocked to learn they may have power they don't even realize. Some years ago, a senator was grappling with an upcoming vote on an amendment that affected two major industries in her state. Billions of dollars were at stake, and one group would win and the other would lose. She later described how she was eventually convinced by one industry leader from her state through a 20-minute conversation they had the day before the vote. She voted his way and the amendment was passed... by one vote. How did this business get access to a U.S. senator the day before a crucial vote? "He reminded my staff that our kids went to the same elementary school together years ago," she said. You or someone in your community or network may have legislative superpowers, and not even know it.

What Hollywood Gets Wrong About Washington

Since the 1970s, public trust in American institutions—including Congress—has steadily declined. Approval ratings for the House and Senate usually hover in the teens. Certainly, some misdeeds by our elected leaders have contributed to this decline and mainstream national media can claim its fair share of "credit" in portraying Congress in a negative light. Yet another major ingredient in the ugly formula poisoning public opinion of Congress is Hollywood. Movies and TV shows routinely portray Congress as craven, corrupt, selfish, and completely indifferent to the public interest. Regrettably, this is a wholly incorrect portrayal of our nation's legislators.

Some years ago, Amazon premiered a TV show, *Alpha House*, loosely based on the true story of four male members of Congress living as roommates in a Washington, D.C. home. The show does have some merit. The depiction of the role of congressional staff is spot on—seemingly subservient to their member in public, but brutally and often profanely honest with them in private. And Bill Murray's cameo in the opening of the pilot just gets funnier every time you watch it. But that's where reality ends.

In one scene a freshman senator agrees to provide a ride to a colleague to visit the home as a prospective new roommate. The senator arrives at the Senate office building in a limousine, drinking champagne with his mistress at his elbow. The truth is the only people who would ride in a limo in Washington are Hollywood types, visiting for some black-tie dinner. Members of Congress are scrupulous about appearances and would never be caught on camera emerging from a fancy car. For years one of the richest senators was Herb Kohl (D-Wisconsin), of the family that founded Kohl's department stores, with a guesstimated net worth of about $500 million. Senator Kohl would only drive a Chevy Lumina—he had one in Washington and one in Milwaukee (identical makes and models).

There are many things Hollywood gets wrong about Washington; here are a few.

What Motivates Congress. While there are certainly self-interested jerks who attain public office, most of Congress is comprised of decent, hardworking public servants. A few years ago, a national polling firm asked Americans if they agreed with this sentence: "Most members of Congress care what their constituents think." Only 11 percent of Americans agreed with that statement (which is probably a scarier number than Congress's low approval rating, since the governing class listening to those they govern is pretty much the bedrock of our democracy). However, in a survey in which members of the U.S. House were asked to rate the most important aspects of their job, 95 percent said "staying in touch with constituents."[7] Members of Congress view it as both their political and moral responsibility to be accountable to their constituents.

How Members of Congress Live. In 1994, not long before he was about to make history as the first speaker of the House of Representatives in 130 years to be ousted in a re-election bid in his home congressional district, Speaker Thomas S. Foley (D-WA) watched a focus group of constituents. The facilitator asked voters in eastern Washington about the life of their congressman. An ironworker described what he thought dinner would be like at a congressman's house: a limousine would take him to a mansion in Georgetown and he would be served a sumptuous meal, eating foods the constituent would not recognize and using utensils the average person would not know how to use.

Foley was stunned. The gap between the constituents' perception and the reality of his daily routine was shocking. He was probably remembering the tuna sandwich he wolfed down for lunch earlier that day, snuck in between 13 meetings over a 14-hour stretch—a common schedule for him and for most members of Congress. While members of Congress are paid more than the average American family, they must maintain two households. Some even sleep in their offices because they cannot afford the steep rent in metropolitan Washington. I once had a most amicable conversation with the House Minority Leader as he was shopping for vegetables at a Washington grocery store. Most members of Congress are a lot more like the head of a typical American family, just trying to balance the challenges of an incredibly hard job with raising a family.

While there have been some fictional portrayals of Congress that have captured Washington correctly,[8] most get it wrong. Former *Washington Post* White House correspondent Juliet Eilperin penned a wonderful

7   Congressional Management Foundation and Society for Human Resource Management, "Life in Congress: The Member Perspective" (2013).
8   The 1990s TV show *The West Wing* most aptly captures what motivates elected officials. The 1960 movie *Advise and Consent* evokes the look, feel, and characters who inhabited the U.S. Senate at the time.

rebuttal to the cynics who revel in distorting Washington. "Many journalists and the officials they cover moved to this town because they care about the ideas and the policies that help shape the world we live in. ... It's why my parents moved here nearly half a century ago, and it's why I have stayed." I'm not saying that the American public does not occasionally send a Frank Underwood to Congress (the devious politician from *House of Cards*). That doesn't change the perhaps boring truth: the vast majority of members of Congress are solid public servants, who sacrifice much for their districts, states, and nation.

2.4. How Legislative Committees Work

Otto von Bismarck, the 19th-century German chancellor, said, "If you like laws or sausages, don't watch how either are made." Congressional committees are the great sausage factories of the legislative process. They are where our elected officials mold language, laws, hope, inspiration, anger, compassion, and their personal views of human nature and society into the rules that we must abide by.

Committees engage in three basic activities: 1) conducting legislative hearings on bills; 2) conducting oversight over the executive branch and societal institutions; and 3) amending and voting on bills.

Legislative Hearings

Capitol Hill hearings have become stages for theater (some might say bad theater) as much as they are components of the legislative process. One committee staff director said, "Conducting a hearing is like directing a play. You write your script, pick your cast, and hope the audience likes it." Hearings allow legislators to gather information on pending legislation or issues, provide a forum for experts and interested parties to voice their knowledge or concern, and allow legislators to probe the impact of one policy or another on the nation.

Hearings also serve as valuable public crucibles, burning down policy questions to their essence. They give victims an opportunity to plead their case, provide space for research to be vetted, and invite public debate.

Organizers of any congressional hearing always consider the public relations impact of the topic and how to attract media interest. They recognize that media coverage can not only enhance the legislator's image, but also highlight their issue and increase public pressure for their cause.

One chairman of the 1990s was seen as a master of the media hearing, even though his subcommittee of the House Small Business Committee was the absolute weakest in Congress and had virtually no legislative jurisdiction. Yet, he found a reason to hold hearings on everything from clinical trials at the National Institutes of Health on breast cancer drugs to questionable marketing tactics by the diet drug industry. He often got media coverage because he scheduled the hearings on Mondays—when other committees didn't hold hearings because legislators didn't return to Washington until Tuesdays for floor votes. The strategy must have had some impact; he's now a senator.

Legislators and staff build a hearing in much the same way a prosecutor builds a criminal case (which isn't surprising, since most of the architects of congressional hearings are lawyers). The chairman picks an issue or piece of legislation that he wishes to highlight or advance; staff then identify and vet potential witnesses to contribute to the topic or narrative and develop logistics for the event. While a specific bill does not have to be the focus of the hearing, the specter of legislation is usually not far away, ensuring the attention of lobbyists and other interest parties.

Oversight Hearings

These are very much like legislative hearings in form except that there need not be a specific bill discussed or even the potential for legislation to be offered. While the Constitution offers no explicit language on Congress's oversight role, the Founders recognized that a system of checks and balances wasn't merely about debating individual legislative proposals. Congress could exercise its power simply by examining and questioning the performance of the president and executive branch in the process of identifying cures to public ills. Over the years, Congress has expanded its oversight role beyond governmental institutions to issues such as tobacco-related public health risks, the proliferation of sexually transmitted diseases among senior citizens, and whether the government should regulate the NCAA.

Even though no legislation may be under consideration, the stakes in oversight and investigatory hearings can be much higher than in legislative hearings. Congress has a powerful weapon to investigate wrongdoing: the subpoena. Chairmen have almost unlimited power to hurl them like thunderbolts at perceived wrongdoers. Witnesses often hire lawyers (since it is a federal crime to lie to Congress), administration personnel hide behind obscure protections to avoid testifying, and the media salivate at the possibility of a public hanging.

Since the advent of television, this process has taken on more meaning and has had a greater impact. Televised hearings have transfixed Americans and shaped public opinion. Examples include Sen. Joe McCarthy's investigation into communism in the early 1950s, the Watergate hearings of the 1970s, and the Iran-Contra hearings of the late 1980s. One of the most recent examples of the power of oversight hearings was the select committee that investigated the events around the January 6, 2021, attack on the Capitol. Regardless of where your opinions fall on those events, the committee was almost universally regarded as a masterful exercise in oversight and storytelling. Not surprisingly, much of the work of crafting the committee hearing narrative was designed by a former producer at ABC News, James Goldston. *The New York Times* described it this way: "More than 20 million Americans watched Mr. Goldston's hand at work during the committee's nationally televised hearing on Thursday evening. They saw tightly edited video of rioters smashing through windows, and two composed witnesses who recounted the destruction and mayhem—viewing that felt more made-for-TV than most congressional hearings."[9]

These and other examples have acted as templates for legislators and staff who seek to right some wrong through public exposure. As Supreme Court Justice Louis Brandeis said, "Sunlight is said to be the best disinfectant."

---

9   Jeremy Peters, "Who Is the Former TV News Chief Helping the Jan. 6 Committee?" *The New York Times*, June 10, 2022.

Amending and Passing Bills

While oversight hearings may be the best congressional theater, the process of amending and passing legislation in congressional committees is more workman-like. It is the legislative process at its core: people offering ideas, debating with colleagues, and compromising to accomplish the achievable.

Legislators have a virtually unlimited opportunity to offer amendments to bills in committee. Because of the difference in House and Senate rules, committees may be the only point in the legislative process where House members can make their mark on a piece of legislation. Any senator can offer any amendment to any bill on the Senate floor. In contrast, House members' amendments must be vetted and approved by the leadership-controlled House Rules Committee before they can be considered on the House floor.

The meeting starts with a proposed bill, and the process is called a "mark-up" (literally meaning to "mark up" the document). Committee members can then offer amendments to the bill. The language may be in legalese, but someone is always around to translate it into English, and most legislators have a firm understanding of what they're voting on. Each amendment is voted up or down, or adopted by "voice vote," meaning there was no recorded vote and it was passed unanimously. In most House committees, votes tend to fall along party lines—but not always.

Finally, chairmen loom large over all subcommittee and committee bill amendment processes. They control the agenda, determine the order in which amendments are considered, and may offer a complete substitute for the scheduled bill (called the "chairman's mark"). Plus, committee members know that they oppose the chairman at their own peril, as any opposition to a chairman's pet bill could result in becoming an outcast—a legislator whose own bills are never considered by the committee. A 2021–2023 analysis of legislative effectiveness found that nine of the ten most successful House Democrats at turning their ideas into law were committee or subcommittee chairs.[10]

10 Craig Volden and Alan Wisemen, "Highlights from the New 117th Congress Legislative Effectiveness Scores," 2023.

Committee Staff

Staffers who work in committees differ from those in members' personal offices in a few ways. They are usually experts in a specific field and are more likely to be older and hold a graduate degree in a related subject. They may have come from the executive branch, providing them valuable insight into the topics and federal agencies they now oversee. They also may be quite bureaucratic in nature, spending decades working on one committee or subcommittee and becoming the pre-eminent experts on recurring legislation that requires regular reauthorization.

Prior to the 1990s, it was common for committee staff to retain their jobs even if control of Congress shifted after an election—chairmen valued staff expertise over partisanship. That practice sadly is no longer the norm, and when the electorate decides it's time to vote one party out of power in the House or Senate, thousands of professional committee staff members begin brushing up their resume the day after the election.

2.5. Congressional Staff Descriptions

With the growth of congressional office staff in the 1960s and 1970s, a predictable organizational chart has developed. These are the titles and roles for congressional staff working in personal offices.

Chief of Staff. This is the head honcho in any congressional office. This person is usually the legislator's closest advisor, and perhaps a long-time friend. They run the operation much like a chief operating officer. (Until the 1990s, this position was known as "administrative assistant.") In the House, chiefs of staff are the top managers in the office. In the Senate, they often play the role of "deputy senator," negotiating deals with other Senate chiefs of staff.

Deputy Chief of Staff. This is a 21st-century addition to the congressional office organizational chart. The title is often combined with another role, so a staffer might have "Deputy Chief of Staff/Legislative Director" on their business card. It's usually bestowed on a senior staff member as a way of communicating their value to the office.

State/District Director. This is the top congressional staffer in the state or district, responsible for managing the operations of the state or district offices. This person usually has the best on-the-ground political skills—frequently a former campaign operative. They oversee the legislator's in-state or in-district schedule and are likely the primary liaison to the groups and individuals key to the legislator's re-election. For large states, senators also have "regional directors."

Legislative Director. Called the "LD," this staffer is the senior policy advisor in the office. She likely has been with the office for more than three or four years, having been promoted from legislative assistant, and now oversees all major policy decisions. The LD usually oversees and edits all new letters and emails drafted by more junior staffers and has jurisdiction over the issues most important to the legislator or most prominent as determined by the legislator's committee assignments.

Legislative Assistant. The "LA" serves as the primary office expert on a particular issue. She drafts statements and speeches, writes memos on legislation, and advises the legislator on the issues in her jurisdiction. In the House, LAs can have up to twelve issues to follow; in the Senate, the range is typically one to ten, depending on the size of the office. House LAs tend to be younger (under 30), while in the Senate they are more likely to have graduate degrees. Those who stick around merit "title bumps"; in the House these staffers are called "senior legislative assistants," while in the Senate they may be promoted to "legislative counsel."

Legislative Correspondent. This staffer, called an "LC," is primarily responsible for managing and drafting responses to mail. Typically, they are very young (under 25) and have less than two years of experience on the Hill. They toil at this thankless job, sorting thousands of emails, postcards, and letters each month, with the hope of being promoted when an LA finds another job. LCs are often assigned non-controversial legislative issues to gain experience working directly with constituents. If you're visiting

Washington and meet with a staffer titled "legislative correspondent," it means it's a very busy day and the LA with jurisdiction had a scheduling conflict.

Systems Administrator. This staffer is responsible for the office's information technology systems and may also have some mail management responsibility. They troubleshoot problems with the computer systems, provide reports to senior staff and the legislator on "mail counts" (who's writing on what), and liaise with institutional offices to ensure the office is up to speed with technological developments and requirements.

Staff Assistant. This staffer primarily answers phone calls and greets visitors. Wise legislators hire someone from the district or state for this job in their Washington office, so that callers feel an instant connection. They are often straight out of college and usually former congressional interns. They also handle requests to purchase American flags that have been flown over the U.S. Capitol (a strange commercial custom still practiced in Congress) and often oversee interns. If you find yourself visiting Washington or calling on an issue, be careful how you treat these impressionable professionals. Today's staff assistant is tomorrow's chief of staff—and one former House staff assistant became a U.S. Senator.[11]

Scheduler. This staffer may also share the title of office manager, and is responsible for the legislator's schedule. Some lawmakers have two schedulers: one in DC and another in the state or district. The scheduler is the ultimate gatekeeper and may determine whether you and your group get to meet with a legislator. In the House, the chief of staff may be the decision maker, but some Senate schedulers are known to make even chiefs of staff cower. They are predominantly women and are super organized. Smart offices hire schedulers who know how to say "no" gracefully. One senator employs a scheduler from the South who is so charming she can reject innumerable requests for a meeting but still make the caller feel he was treated like a king.

---

11 Blanche Lambert started working as a staff assistant for her Arkansas congressman, Bill Alexander, right out of college in 1982. In 1992 she challenged her former boss in a Democratic primary and beat him 60 percent to 40 percent. In 1996 she ran for and won a U.S. Senate seat, making her the first former staff assistant to rise to U.S. Senator.

Caseworker/Field Representative. This staffer's primary responsibility is to respond to requests from constituents and to act as a liaison or advocate in solving problems, mostly involving a federal agency. Each office has an elaborate system for reviewing and tracking these requests. The caseworker usually has a network of contacts with federal agencies that allows them to cut through red tape. These staffers also may attend functions on behalf of the legislator, conveying her position on key issues and reporting back to the office with relevant insights.

Press Secretary/Communications Director. This staffer manages the legislator's public relations. House offices usually have one person dedicated to the job, while Senate offices can have up to five communications staff, depending upon the size of the state. Press secretaries write press releases, liaise with reporters, oversee the website, draft speeches, and advise the legislator on the public relations impact of decisions.

Digital Director. With the advent of social media, congressional offices shifted resources and added a staffer to manage platforms like Facebook, X (formerly Twitter), and Instagram. They are often very tech-savvy and have an eye for which member activity or messaging might go viral on social media.

Intern. I'm always disappointed when a young person, asked by a constituent what she does in the office, replies, "I'm just an intern." The reality is that Capitol Hill would grind to a halt without the thousands of people who comprise this enthusiastic and inexpensive labor force. Interns open the mail, answer the phones, conduct guided tours of the Capitol building for constituent groups, and sometimes even cover hearings. I conducted dozens of intern training programs for the House of Representatives, and each time, just before casting these fresh young minds into three months of administrative servitude, I reminded them they weren't "just" interns, and told them this story.

In 2001, Jennifer Luciano was an intern for Rep. Danny Davis (D-Illinois). While conducting constituent tours of the U.S. Capitol Building, she noticed something: there were no statues recognizing the role of African

American women in the suffragette movement. Jennifer noted this absence to Congressman Davis's chief of staff, who in turn passed it on to the congressman, who said, "You're right, we ought to do something about this." So, on June 20, 2001, with her mother and grandfather in attendance, Jennifer was recognized at a press conference on the grounds of the U.S. Capitol as Congressman Danny Davis introduced H. Con. Res 169, "Directing the Architect of the Capitol to enter into a contract for the design and construction of a monument to commemorate the contributions of minority women to women's suffrage and to the participation of women in public life, and for other purposes." Eight years later a statue of Black American Sojourner Truth took its place beside Washington, Jackson, and Jefferson. Being "just an intern" sometimes means more than opening the mail.

2.6. Individual Members of Congress Have More Power Than You Realize

Most Americans' impression of what Congress does is limited to watching the C-SPAN view of the House and Senate floor as members of Congress cast their votes. But floor activity and votes generally show Congress in its least powerful and meaningful role. In reality, even members in the minority party wield significant influence over public policy and can offer substantial help to their constituents. Below is a menu of options and services to request of your elected officials.

Legislative Chamber Floor Activity

Cosponsor a Bill. The most common way members of Congress support a colleague's legislation is by cosponsoring a bill. This simple act is a demonstration of support for the legislation. Whether the lawmaker responds positively to the request usually depends on a variety of factors. Does the legislation cost a lot of money? Are constituents in the district affected by the bill? Has the bill been referred to a committee the member serves on? Some offices, to demonstrate their bipartisanship, will only add cosponsors if they can get an equal number from both parties to cosponsor. Yet, constituent requests remain by far the most common reason lawmakers cosponsor bills. One chief of staff said, "If we get a constituent who asks us to sign onto a letter or cosponsor a bill, if it's not controversial, 99 percent of the time we'll do it. The constituent often knows more about the issue than my boss."

Floor Amendment. House and Senate members can propose amendments to bills pending in their chambers. For House members, the House Rules Committee must allow their amendment to be offered up for a vote on the House floor. Technically, senators have unlimited power to offer amendments. However, recent practices in the Senate require a "unanimous consent agreement" whereby all senators agree to a list of amendments to be considered and a reasonable time limit for debate and voting.

One-Minute Speech. When the House and Senate began televising their proceedings in the 1980s, Congress became at times more of a theater than a legislative body. As such, the House of Representatives created the "one-minute speech," allowing any member to make remarks at the beginning of the daily session if it does not exceed 60 seconds. This has resulted in both good and bad television. (One member, to convey the shame he felt for the institution during a congressional scandal, gave his speech with a paper bag over his head.[12]) Citizen-advocates can ask their representative to highlight their issue using this opportunity.

Special Order. When House members wish to give extra attention to an issue they can request and schedule a "Special Order"—a block of time reserved for speeches delivered after the House has concluded its legislative business for the day. There is no limit on their length or how many members of the House can speak. House members usually coordinate with colleagues to give a series of speeches, which are broadcast on C-SPAN, highlighting legislation or an issue. Even though the chamber is empty, the camera—

---

12 In order to demonstrate his shame over the unfolding scandal involving members of Congress using the unique House bank to float overdrafts in 1991, Rep. Jim Nussle (R-Iowa) put a paper bag over his head as he delivered his rebuke.

controlled by the House of Representatives, not C-SPAN—shows the member at the center of the august chamber.

In the early 1990s, then-backbench Rep. Newt Gingrich famously used this tactic before he rose to power as speaker to rile his colleagues and hammer at the Democratic majority. A perturbed Speaker Tip O'Neill briefly combatted this display by ordering the House camera operators to show that Gingrich was speaking to an empty chamber. A bipartisan compromise soon followed: the camera would remain fixed on the speaker during Special Orders so as not to embarrass colleagues in this way.

Committee Activity

Committee Amendment. The most common legislative vehicle for House and Senate members is to offer an amendment to a bill at the committee level. When legislators meet in committee to consider a bill, the process of voting on amendments is known as a "markup," whereby lawmakers are literally "marking up" or editing a piece of legislation. Despite some improvements to modernize Congress, this process has been largely unchanged throughout its history.[13] Convincing a member of Congress to offer an amendment in support of a particular cause or issue is a great achievement for a citizen-advocate.

Bill Report Language. Nearly every bill that is passed by the House or Senate is accompanied by a report—largely written by staff—that amplifies, clarifies, or expands upon the language in the legislation. While the report language does not have the power of law, in some cases courts have examined and referenced bill report language to determine the efficacy or constitutionality of the legislation. Convincing committee staff to insert certain phrases or language into a bill report is easier than getting a bill or amendment passed in committee because it does not require a majority vote of the committee, merely the consent of senior committee staff and sometimes the committee chair. This may sound nefarious and richly undemocratic, and sometimes

---

13 In recent years, committees of the U.S. House of Representatives have installed electronic voting technology, significantly improving the efficiency of committee votes.

language which benefits one special interest group does make its way into bill report language. However, most of the time language is inserted to urge or guide an executive branch agency on how the committee wishes to see the legislation implemented.

Field Hearings. Sometimes Congress takes its "show on the road" by holding an official committee hearing outside of the Capitol Hill campus; these are known as "field hearings." House and Senate members often conduct field hearings to garner local media attention on an issue or bill and allow constituents to go on the record before a congressional committee. Though often attended by just one or two committee members, field hearings are official proceedings of Congress, and carry the same weight and legal authority of a hearing held in Washington, D.C. For citizen-advocates, they offer a powerful opportunity to highlight their issue and build a record before Congress.

Witness Testimony. Members of Congress often invite constituents to testify before their committees—either because they are experts in their field or because they have a compelling story to tell about how a particular policy affected them, their family, or their community. Congress will even sometimes cover the cost of travel to Washington to testify before a congressional committee. Those selected should expect significant prep-time with committee staff, as they will seek to create a narrative and want the member of Congress's constituent portrayed in the best light.

Hearing Questions. In recent years, congressional committee hearings have devolved into bad reality TV shows, whereby the committee members are more interested in scoring political or media points than debating the finer details of public policy. Yet, citizen-advocates can use this development to their advantage by coaxing their lawmakers to ask certain questions at hearings. Members of Congress and their staffs are often not deeply familiar with the legislation they consider in committees and rely on outside experts to help them prepare for hearings. If a citizen-advocate learns that an issue or bill is going to be discussed at a committee hearing, they should propose questions to be asked of witnesses. Congressional staff are often harried and overworked, and usually welcome even unsolicited suggestions for hearing questions.

Inserting Language in the "Chairman's Mark." If you remember the wonderful cartoon, "I'm Just a Bill," it suggests that once a bill is voted on in committee it heads to the House floor unchanged for a final vote. But sometimes our little "Bill" gets a bit of a makeover before he hits the floor. Committee chairs wield almost dictatorial power to alter legislation coming from their committee, a practice known as the "Chairman's Mark." Even after a bill passes committee, lobbyists or constituents can request provisions be added to the legislation before it is voted on by the full House or Senate. The Affordable Care Act of 2011 ("Obamacare") was voted on by multiple House and Senate committees. Yet the final piece of legislation was largely crafted by the staff of Speaker Nancy Pelosi, in coordination with other Democratic congressional committee chairs. It usually requires some degree of legislative knowledge and an existing relationship with committee staff to pull off this achievement, but it is doable.

Influencing the Executive Branch

The executive branch is bound both politically and constitutionally to listen to and respond to the legislative branch. In an era of divided government, the minority party in Congress still may retain the White House and have some influence over federal agencies. Often, the official receiving the request is a nonpartisan civil servant who will be equally responsive no matter which party is asking.

Pressure Agencies. Occasionally, members of Congress will apply pressure on federal agencies to change public policy on behalf of a group of constituents. It usually starts with a rather bureaucratic or legalistic letter written by a congressional staffer (with the legislator's signature) and sent to a cabinet secretary or other senior agency official. If the legislator genuinely wants to see the action happen, there will be follow-up phone calls and the occasional threat of a departmental funding cut to induce the agency official to act.

Some years ago, Wisconsin constituents approached their U.S. senator at the summer state fair to complain about a new fuel additive introduced by the Environmental Protection Agency (EPA). The additive was better for the environment but was wrecking their lawn mower and chainsaw two-cycle engines. Now, if you prevent someone in Green Bay from mowing their lawn in August, that's a mild problem. But come January, and Wisconsinites find that the federal government is screwing up their snowmobiles (which also operate with two-cycle engines), you've got a potential political riot on your hands. The senator got the message and successfully pressured the EPA to change the fuel mix formula to not disable chainsaws, lawn mowers, and snowmobiles. No law was passed, and no federal regulation was proposed or adopted. Just a pressure campaign emanating from constituents, via a U.S. senator. As the great Senator Everett Dirksen (D-Illinois) once said, "When I feel the heat, I see the light."

Requesting a Government Research Report. A great method to influence public policy is to develop solid research to support the cause. One of the most beneficial, but least heralded government entities is the U.S. Government Accountability Office (GAO). Basically, the GAO is the government's auditor. When people hear about the government rooting out "waste, fraud, and abuse," there's usually some wonky GAO staffer behind it. And these aren't just some nerdy reports. In 2023 GAO work yielded $70.4 billion in financial benefits for Congress and the American people. Those reports usually start with a request from a group of members of Congress, and often there is a constituent or stakeholder group behind the idea for the research, such as a trade association or nonprofit the constituents belong to. It's a proven strategy for shining a light on a problem, need, or aspirational goal.

Communications

Whether in the majority or minority, members of Congress have a myriad of communications tools available to them, all funded by taxpayers. They use these tools to influence other legislators, communicate to the media, and demonstrate their value to constituents.

Dear Colleague Letters. One method that a member of Congress can use to gin up support from colleagues for a bill or issue is to distribute a "Dear Colleague Letter." These brief, one- to two-page letters are distributed to every member office in that chamber. They are often written in plain language, asking their colleagues to support a cause, issue, or pending legislation. Sometimes the Dear Colleagues are signed by many members of Congress so that the supporters can demonstrate the breadth of support. Citizen-advocates who participate with their trade association or support a nonprofit may be asked by that group to reach out to their lawmakers, asking they sign on to the letter.

Social Media. Platforms like X or Facebook are solid tools for engaging with an elected official. By teaming up with a lawmaker, advocates can reach millions of people. Senator Bernie Sanders (D-Vermont) has more than 20 million followers on X. Consider that for a moment; when Senator Sanders tweets about an issue or shows a photograph of a constituent, that issue or person is being presented to tens of millions of people. Constituents are encouraged to get photos with their lawmakers, then post about it from their own account and *include the lawmaker's handle*. There's a good chance the legislator will repost it to their massive base of followers.

Website. An elected official's website has become the end-all-be-all for their work. Great congressional websites can be wonderful tools of accountability for constituents if the legislator makes a commitment to be transparent and comprehensive. They include detailed voting records, specific statements on their positions on key issues, and information about how the congressional office can assist constituents with problems stemming from federal agencies. Alternatively, bad websites look like campaign commercials, simply touting what the press secretary thinks will promote the boss.

Press Release. The press release—which traces its origin to the early 20th century—is still a primary medium for congressional communications. For major activity by the legislator, press releases can act as sort of a "database of record," chronicling the most important projects, positions, or legislation championed by the member of Congress.

A Shocking Example of Congressional Effectiveness

Most Americans think Congress is broken, and why wouldn't they? The portrayal of our legislative branch in mainstream media and Hollywood is abysmal. That makes it all the more shocking and worthy of celebration when we see the institution actually getting something done. This is a case study in congressional effectiveness: the Select Committee on the Modernization of Congress.

In 2019, the U.S. House of Representatives took on an unexpected and daunting challenge: how to improve itself. In a bipartisan manner it formed a Select Committee on the Modernization of Congress with a simple but ambitious mandate: to "promote a more modern and efficient Congress."

Chaired by Rep. Derek Kilmer (D-Washington), the committee broke the mold in many ways. First, despite a Democratic majority in the House, it had an equal number of Democrats and Republicans. Second, all recommendations required a two-thirds approval to pass, meaning all recommendations needed to be bipartisan. The committee also did something few committees do: to establish their procedures and process they held a full-day retreat for their members. This author had the opportunity to witness this event in 2019 and can attest to this: if every American could see how these lawmakers interacted in a genuine, honest, and constructive way, they would have a very different view of Congress. "We actually spent time together, and we talked about things," said William Timmons (R-South Carolina), vice chair of the committee.

In every facet of its operation, the Select Committee on Modernization defied convention and pulled down partisan barriers. Instead of using the traditional hearing room dais to sit above their witnesses and audience, they all sat around a table together. Instead of two partisan staffs, they had one bipartisan staff. At hearings they didn't divide into two camps, but instead sat next to each other, Democrat next to Republican. Amanda Ripley, an expert on conflict resolution, testified before the committee. "I'd covered a lot of hearings as a reporter, and they always felt choreographed, stilted and performative. This experience was different," she said. "It felt, at times, like members were sharing their genuine fears and asking real questions. It was not obvious who was on which political side, which was at once both disorienting and wonderful."[14]

The Committee was so successful that its one-year mandate was extended—first to two years, then again through 2023. Their

---

14 Amanda Ripley, "These radically simple changes helped lawmakers actually get things done," *The Washington Post,* February 9, 2023.

accomplishments include increasing pay for congressional staff, which had been stagnant for a decade; enhancing professional development of staff; and creating a novel information technology department to launch new tools for House offices. More than 200 recommendations were passed by the committee, with most of them moving to implementation within a year. "If all of Congress could operate the way that the modernization committee has, the nation would be in a much better place," committee member Rep. Emanuel Cleaver II (D-Missouri) said.

Among their most significant accomplishments was renewing and reforming the system for congressional earmarks—projects specifically requested by a community and championed by a member of Congress. This system fell into disrepute some years ago because of questionable projects (remember the "bridge to nowhere"?), and Republicans banned earmarks in 2011. Yet this throw-the-baby-out-with-the-bathwater strategy inadvertently shifted more power over federal spending decisions from the legislative branch to the executive branch, in blatant disregard of Article I of the Constitution and the intentions of our Founders. The new system was limited, as members could request only ten projects a year; transparent, in that all requests needed to be made public; and more focused on the public good, as funding could not be bestowed on private companies.

In 2020, Rep. Rosa DeLauro (D-Connecticut), chair of the House Appropriations Committee, adopted the system under a new name: "Community Funded Projects." The Senate quickly followed with their own process, and Republicans kept the system largely in place when they gained the majority in 2023. There are new bridges, roads, hospital wings, police headquarters, and many other community projects throughout the nation because of the work of the Select Committee on Modernization. Collectively, the committee's recommendations will strengthen Congress, allow constituents to have a greater voice in government, and lead to better service to, and representation of, the American people.

While the full committee's formal mandate ended in early 2023, House Republican leadership recognized its value and created a new Subcommittee on Modernization. The subcommittee became the institutional implementer of the recommendations and continues its mandate of improving America's premiere democratic institution.

Chapter 3
How Lawmakers Make Decisions

In a republic, it is not the people themselves who make the decisions, but the people they themselves choose to stand in their places.

— James Madison

Despite the efforts of high school social studies teachers, parents, journalists, and political scientists, the workings of our government remain a mystery to most Americans. More people can name the seven dwarfs than can name a member of the U.S. Supreme Court. Caricatures, misconceptions, and stereotypes dominate citizens' view of Congress, which contributes to our reluctance to get involved in our democracy. In reality, the system works pretty much as we were taught in third grade. Congress is far more like *Schoolhouse Rock* than *House of Cards*.

By design, the American Congress is slow and deliberative. The Founders created it in reaction to a monarchy that was quick to impose authoritarian rule on the colonists, often with unpleasant consequences. So, in 1789, the new government was structured with an elaborate system of checks and balances to ensure that no branch or part of government could dominate the process or the citizen. While this is at times frustrating, it is the fundamental reason why the United States has endured for more than 230 years (and many other governments have not).

Individual legislators must wrestle with this deliberative system, blending their own beliefs into a legislative melting pot that, ideally, produces positive societal outcomes. They use a kind of political math to make decisions, weighing multiple factors when determining whether to vote for a bill, cosponsor legislation, or support funding for an initiative. When all the details are burned away, legislators generally follow three voices when making a decision. One member of Congress called these voices the "Three H's": Heart, Head, and Health—meaning political health.

3.1. Heart

People who make decisions that affect the lives and well-being of others are usually first guided by their own beliefs and value system. When asked how he made decisions, a GOP House lawmaker said, "I'm guided by the values my parents taught me. What's the most common sense, ethical way to solve the problem?" Legislators genuinely wrestle with difficult decisions, especially at a time when the country is so deeply divided.

There's no directory that lists which legislators are mostly guided by their conscience and which are motivated by other factors. Generally, senators— who enjoy six-year terms—are expected to demonstrate a "leadership" model of decision-making, sometimes bucking public opinion. This is by design: the Senate was intended to be a more deliberative, thoughtful institution, acting as a check on the House, which could be swayed by the hot passions of the public. Of course, this principle tends to erode the closer a senator gets to re-election (funny how that works).

(The Founders' original constitutional design pushed senators even farther from the public by having them elected by state legislatures. That system was changed in 1913 with the adoption of the 17th Amendment to the Constitution, which allowed voters to directly elect senators.)

In the House, more senior members who are in "safe" seats with little danger of losing re-election are more inclined to follow their own counsel rather than other pressures.

3.2. Head

Working in Congress is a policy wonk's dream. You have access to *every* study ever written, *every* expert in the country, *every* federal, state, and local agency. And if that is not enough, the largest library in the world—the Library of Congress—is across the street from your office. Most legislators and staff *love* doing research on public policy problems. This is why they chose this career—to analyze difficult issues and develop an approach or solution to improve the human condition.

Legislators are constantly hunting for unbiased, independent research to help them make decisions. There is both a practical and political reason for this: in addition to guiding their thinking, independent studies that justify a policy also provide them with political cover. A member of Congress told me that he had changed his position on the issue of climate change, from opposing mandatory caps on emissions to supporting them. Since he represented a coal-producing district, I asked him what contributed to his change in thinking. "I read the 300-page United Nations study on the topic," he said. Many legislators are policy wonks—that's often the real reason they run for public office. They study issues, interpret data, and determine the best public policy based on their analysis. One member of Congress had a "to read" pile that was *four feet high*. She would often forgo sleep ("Four hours a night is OK sometimes," she would say) to gain a complete understanding of an issue.

Chart 1 Survey of Congressional Staff

How frequently do messages from constituents include the following?

How helpful is it for messages from constituents to include the following?

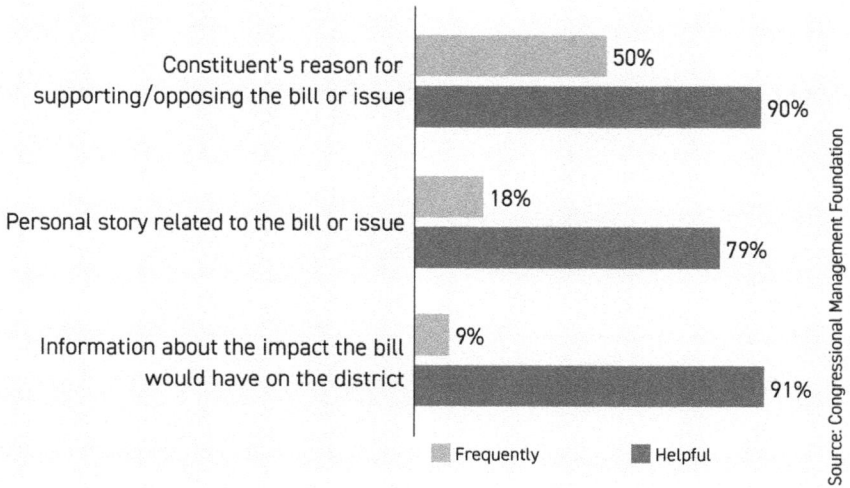

Source: Congressional Management Foundation

3.3. Health (political)

Politics is often considered a dirty word, but what citizens and pundits fail to realize is that when a legislator factors "politics" into a decision, it means they are *listening to constituents.* Usually, a legislator's personal beliefs and the general attitudes of his constituency are not far apart—that is why he got elected. Yet most decisions do not affect a majority of the citizenry in a district or state; they tend to impact small groups in significant ways. For example, Medicare reimbursement rates primarily impact doctors, research funding for a particular disease affects those afflicted with the illness, and visa limits for high-skilled foreign workers concern technology companies.

There may be major issues—such as war in the Middle East or climate change—which engender opinions in nearly everyone. But those issues are rare in the day-to-day world of government. Most decisions affect a narrow class of people, which makes the politics easy to assess. When faced with a new issue, one House chief of staff said he first asks, "Who's for it, who's against it?"

There are many ways legislators assess the political impact of a decision, but for each one they will conduct a political analysis of how it impacts voters' perceptions in their district or state and how it might affect their next election. It's important to note that even legislators in safe districts are very much swayed by constituents' views. This is for two reasons. First, they feel an ethical responsibility to honestly represent the people who elected them (it sounds corny, but they do). Second, every politician wants to be loved by everyone—that's part of why they went into politics. For better or worse, legislators sometimes measure their self-worth by their election margin, and anything that could drop them below 60 percent will give them heartburn. One representative told me, "I sometimes think that every member of Congress is a middle child who is still trying to please his father."

The notion that legislators are guided by these three factors—heart, head, and health—defies the popular (and cynical) belief that other influences are the "real" reason behind legislative behavior. Yet both anecdotal evidence and survey research support this conclusion. In 2023, the Congressional Management Foundation conducted an extensive survey of congressional staff. According to staff, the factors that most influenced an undecided legislator were: 1) constituent meetings, whether in-person or virtual; 2) contact from anyone who represents many constituents, such as a nonprofit leader, state association president, or large employer; and 3) personally written messages. (See Chart 3 in Section 5.4 for details.)

This collision between cynical popular belief and the reality of public service became clear to me in the most surprising setting: talking to congressional interns. During my 13 years on Capitol Hill, I always supervised the interns in the office. And at the end of their three-month tenure, I always asked the same question: "What belief or stereotype about Washington or Congress was debunked during your time here?" The most common response went something like this: "I was surprised by how much you all wrestle with trying to do the right thing, and how much you worry about the impact of your decisions on constituents." If you spend a little time in the real Washington—not the one shown on the front pages or in movies—you'll come to the same conclusion.

Finally, any analysis of what goes into legislative decision-making would be incomplete without addressing a prevalent belief in our society: that members of Congress don't know what's in the bills they vote on. While it is true that the rare provision helping one group or another can be tucked into massive bills without the knowledge of most legislators or staff, members of Congress are generally well educated on what they're voting on. They usually don't read the legislative language; they have lawyers to do that. Instead, they read accurate, detailed summaries or other reports created by a vast army of researchers working in and out of Congress. It's nonsense to think that political creatures are going to guess their way through their jobs when their professional survival is dependent on how their votes are interpreted by the media, key stakeholders, and constituents. Members of Congress take pains to understand exactly what they're doing when they vote "yea" or "nay" on any bill before them.

Chapter 4
People Who Can and Can't Influence Legislators and How They Do It

Look at my arms, you will find no party hand-cuff on them.
— **Rep. Davy Crockett (National Republican-Tennessee)**

As noted throughout this book, constituents usually dominate legislators' decision-making. But just as you would consult multiple sources before making a big decision, members of Congress do the same thing. They turn to family, friends, people they work with, and experts on the topic.

4.1. Family and Friends Have the Lawmaker's Ear

In the 2008 Democratic primary battle between Senators Hillary Clinton and Barack Obama, Senator Bob Casey (D-Pennsylvania) said that a factor in his decision to endorse Obama was pressure from his four daughters.

A few years ago, an organizer with the Alzheimer's Association was attending one of their annual "Walk to End Alzheimer's," which often attract members of Congress. The organizer was delighted to meet their U.S. senator and his spouse. But she also noted when they met, "I wish we could get your Senate colleague to join us on one of these walks." Before the senator could reply, his spouse jumped in: "What? He's not here?" The organizer soon learned the senator's strong support for Alzheimer's research funding emanated from his wife, whose mother died of the disease. Before the walk was over, the organizer got an email from the *other* senator's state director, requesting a meeting between the senator and local constituents who volunteered for the cause. It appears the first senator's wife immediately called the second senator's wife; they were good friends. Because of the spousal connection, the national nonprofit had a new champion in the U.S. Senate. You don't have to be experts on a topic to have influence. You just have to have the ear of a member of Congress and be someone they trust.

4.2. Knowledgeable Acquaintances Can Make a Difference

Politicians know a *lot* of people. Some folks claim to be "a friend of the congressman" when they maybe saw him once at some charity event. One lawmaker estimated that 2,000 people had his personal cell phone number. (He spent a lot of time answering his cell phone.) When these acquaintances have knowledge of a particular topic, they can be very influential, as they may be tagged "expert" and "friend" by the member of Congress—a powerful combination. "What also really works is when I get calls from individual supporters that I know and respect," said one senator. "They'll call me and say, 'I've known you for years and I know this issue.' I listen to that."

These acquaintances take many forms. Perhaps they used to work in the same company or belong to the same club or place of worship. The important part is that they are a "stakeholder" to the elected officials—someone who can get access to their time and attention. This is why mapping out a lawmaker's relationships is a key part of advanced citizen-advocacy. Good advocates do a little research, identifying groups or individuals who may have a connection to the lawmaker. If the constituent has a similar connection (e.g., they are members of the same church) they can use that connection to talk to the lawmaker. Politicians are *joiners* and often use their organizational affiliations for political advantage. The reverse can also work—people who belong to those same groups can use that affiliation to meet with elected officials.

A few years ago, in a focus group with senior congressional staff, participants were asked why one group, the National Association of Realtors, was so influential. A senior U.S. Senate aide answered, "For all I know, that realtor I'm meeting with might have sold my boss his first home." And the connection doesn't even have to be a recent one. One major lobbyist in Washington said this: "A congresswoman's twelfth grade social studies teacher probably has more influence on her than all the lobbyists in Washington." Connections in politics are a significant factor in who does and does not get an audience with an elected official.

4.3. Legislators Pay Attention to Respected Colleagues

There was once a freshmen member of Congress who, when confronted with a tough decision on military matters, would ask, "How is Les Aspin voting on this?" Rep. Aspin (D-WI) was the chairman of the Armed Services Committee (1985–1993) and later served as Secretary of Defense under President Bill Clinton. He was by all accounts one of the most brilliant minds on military policy of his generation. Sometimes legislators seek guidance from expert legislators who have studied an issue and bring a politician's perspective to the debate. Junior members of a congressional delegation may wait to see how the "dean of the delegation" (the state's most senior member) will vote before determining their position. And rarely, members of Congress will have no idea how they're going to vote on an issue until they walk onto the House floor and observe how an influential colleague has voted.

4.4. Legislative Leaders, Arm Twisting, and the Power (or not) of the Party

The public holds an inflated view of the power of congressional leadership. Most think that all members of Congress simply do what they're told by their party leaders. And it is true that especially in recent years, on major issues, the power pendulum has probably swung too far towards leadership, especially in the U.S. House. Yet, for most issues, leadership plays a less influential role in guiding the day-to-day decisions of most members of Congress. The nadir of leadership power was probably the ouster of Speaker Kevin McCarthy (R-CA) in 2023 by just a few Republican malcontents in the U.S. House (and with the unanimous support of every House Democrat).

Especially in the Senate, personal relationships and just old-fashioned political horse-trading are usually more influential for most legislative matters. When Republicans were pushing a repeal of the Affordable Care Act, leadership definitely took notice of defectors and pushed to exact a price for nonconformity. And, as noted in Section 2.4, committee chairs expect party unity on committee votes, especially on bills favored by the chair. But when it comes to cosponsoring legislation advocated by constituents, or advocating before a federal agency on a regulation, rank-and-file members of Congress generally are free to use their own judgement and do what they think is best for their district or state.

4.5. The Real Influence of Lobbyists

The popular portrayal of lobbyists as shadowy figures controlling the government is largely inaccurate. Most lobbyists in Washington don't drive fancy cars, don't have expense accounts, and don't work for "fat-cat" corporations. Moreover, they don't determine policy outcomes—organized citizens do.

In reality, most lobbyists are professional advocates who believe in their cause and understand the details of an issue, whether it be finding a cure for diabetes, improving the environment, or opposing new taxes that could cause businesses to lay off workers. Most people in Washington who make their livelihoods as professional advocates don't work for lobbying firms at all. They work for associations, nonprofits, and companies representing millions of Americans affiliated with their organizations. The influence they wield is not with money. Their power is their knowledge of a topic, their ability to communicate it effectively, and their skill in assessing how a decision will affect a lawmaker's state or district. "Lobbyists can often be clear, concise, and compelling," said one House chief of staff. "Plus, we can hold them accountable. Sometimes that's hard to do with a constituent."

The roles and influence of lobbyists was summed up best by Jeffrey H. Birnbaum of *The Washington Post,* one of the leading reporters on the intersection of special interests and policymaking. "Lobbying is much more substantive and out in the open than its ugly caricature," Birnbaum wrote. "Lobbyists primarily woo lawmakers with facts. Making the case is what effective lobbyists do most and best. They spend the rest of their time persuading lawmakers' constituents to back the same causes, very much in the mode of an electoral campaign. If members of Congress see merit in a position and there is a public outcry in its favor, that's the way they tend to vote." [15]

---

15 Jeffrey Birnbaum, "Mickey Goes to Washington," *The Washington Post*, February 17, 2008.

Chart 2 Survey of Congressional Staff

If your Member has not arrived at a firm decision on an issue, approximately how many email messages from people who represent many constituents (e.g., organization leader, elected official, business owner) does it take for your office to consider taking the action requested?

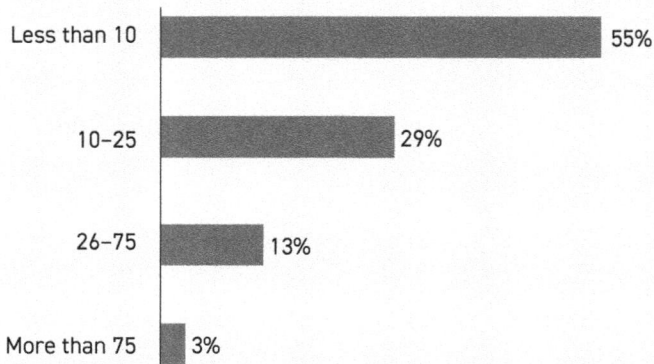

Source: Congressional Management Foundation

Less than 10	55%
10–25	29%
26–75	13%
More than 75	3%

4.6. What Legislators Want from Lobbyists vs. Constituents

Legislators at every level of government rely on both constituents and lobbyists to help them make decisions. The best way to think about their respective roles is to refer to them as "citizen-advocates" (constituents) and "professional-advocates" (lobbyists). Understanding how lawmakers and their staff utilize each group's knowledge and input will aid in influencing public policy.

Scope of Expertise

Professional-advocates are subject matter experts on a particular policy or area of legislation. They can usually convey the national implications of a public policy decision. The caricature of the sleazy lobbyist plying lawmakers with liquor and lavish meals is a relic of the past.

Citizen-advocates, by contrast, are at their best when communicating the impact of a public policy decision on a *local* level. Legislators crave detailed information about how their decisions will affect a group of constituents— for both political and ethical reasons. If a policy or law negatively affects a community, and that lawmaker missed the signs it was coming, it could mean the end of their political career. Constituents who can describe how a group or a community would be affected by a bill or issue are crucial to elected officials' decision-making. "Constituents are easier for getting the tone and feeling of the district and have a wider focus than lobbyists," said a House chief of staff.

Type of Content Delivered

Professional-advocates in Washington, D.C., are often former congressional staff who have amassed years of experience on a topic and usually know more about it than the members of Congress and staff they meet with. They produce policy reports, spreadsheets, and other tools legislators and their staff can reference in a policy discussion.

The best citizen-advocates are storytellers, making the emotional argument rather than the rational one. Research on both the psychology and neuroscience of persuasion concludes that stories are more impactful to listeners than spreadsheets and charts. By putting a face on an issue, the citizen-advocate makes the policy pitch real in a way that a professional-advocate cannot. "I've seen my boss change his mind because of a personal story," said one House chief of staff.

Potential Coalition Allies

Smart professional-advocates wrangle other groups to support their cause or bill. The more diverse the coalition, the better. Sometimes churches or religious groups—typically known for their stances on cultural issues— will team up with anti-poverty nonprofits to champion more funding for food assistance programs. If a politician can say "yes" once and make two stakeholders happy, they gladly accept that math.

Citizen-advocates have the potential to build allies and coalitions at the local level, sometimes using their network as a power source. While the local nonprofit food bank may serve the most vulnerable in its community, the chair of its board of directors could be president of the local chamber of commerce. If citizen-advocates combine their request with a friend's in the community, the elected official is much more likely to take notice.

Activating a Network

It is the full-time job of a professional-advocate to monitor the legislative environment for key developments, such as the introduction of a bill or an important committee meeting. When those developments are discovered, they'll alert their membership or stakeholder group and ask constituents to weigh in, hoping to influence lawmakers. This is often done through grassroots software, and citizen-advocates need to register with the trade association or nonprofit to receive these "Action Alerts." When an alert hits your inbox, you should act immediately. And as noted in Chart 3 in Chapter 5, every message sent to a lawmaker must be personalized or localized to have maximum impact.

4.7. Campaign Contributors Are Less Influential Than You Think

There's a dirty secret in Washington that neither Congress nor the special interest community want to get out: campaign contributions really don't influence legislative outcomes all that much. The reality is that a high-dollar campaign contributor will likely get access to a legislator—perhaps a returned phone call from the member or his senior staff. However, the average constituent can get the same access with about the same amount of effort by showing up at a town hall meeting, or organizing an in-person meeting with three or four like-minded constituents in the legislator's Washington or district office.

A chief of staff was asked to gauge who had more influence: someone who gave his boss $1,000 in campaign contributions, or a constituent who had flown to Washington for a meeting with the congressman. His reply, "About the same—it just depends on who makes the best argument." Keep in mind that with the skyrocketing costs of campaigns, and the strict limits imposed by new campaign finance laws, a $1,000 contribution represents a tiny fraction of what the lawmaker must raise for his re-election effort. One House member from a competitive district said, "A mistake that critics make is that they overestimate the role of money and underestimate the power of the threat of the next election."

The reality is that constituent views often outweigh those of campaign contributors. Rep. Barney Frank (D-Massachusetts) was the longtime chairman of the House Financial Services Committee, a veritable vacuum for campaign contributions. In an interview he noted the power of constituent views. "As chairman of a committee, I'd be lobbying for votes," he said. "I have had members say to me, 'Mr. Chairman, I love you. Barney, you're right. But I can't do that politically because I'll get killed in my district.' No one has ever said to me, 'I'm sorry, but I got a big contributor I can't offend.'"[16]

4.8. Legislators and Polling

Legislators read polls about everything: their approval rating, their re-election prospects, the mood of the district, how voters prioritize issues, and even which exact words or phrases resonate best in their campaigns. It varies from legislator to legislator—and from issue to issue—as to whether polls influence their decision-making.

For example, a member of Congress may generally think a trade agreement with another country is in the best long-term interests of the nation, but if he represents a union-dominated district that is overwhelmingly opposed, he might follow public opinion polling. In contrast, when legislators make

16 Ira Glass, "Take the Money and Run for Office," *This American Life*, March 30, 2012.

decisions about whether to send the nation to war, I don't know of a single member of Congress who didn't search deep in her soul for the right answer and generally ignore public polling. Polls are sometimes singled out as a major influence on lawmakers' decision-making, and they are certainly used by lawmakers to gauge public opinion (especially close to elections). However, they are but one of many factors that legislators consider.

4.9. How Paid Advertising Affects Legislators' Thinking

Occasionally, interest groups will purchase television, radio, print, or Internet advertising (called "paid media"). There are two categories of advocacy advertising: 1) ads genuinely intended to influence the decision-making of a member of Congress near a crucial vote by swaying public opinion in her state; and 2) ads timed around elections, created to appear like advocacy messages but really intended to influence voters about to head to the polls. Messages of the campaign variety will include numerous attacks on the legislator's opinions, voting record, or character—and conclude with the line, "Send a message to Representative Smith." (The unstated assumption is that the "message" is a one-way ticket out of Congress.) These ads are designed to influence election outcomes rather than policy. Numerous rulings by the U.S. Supreme Court have established that these messages are not covered under federal campaign finance laws—meaning that citizens have no way of knowing who pays for them.

In some legislative battles, interested parties will pay for advertising in a legislator's state with the goal of generating a groundswell of support for their position. They hope it will translate into calls, emails, and letters to the congressional office. One of the best examples of this occurred in 1994, when the "Harry and Louise" ads targeted members of Congress vulnerable for re-election. They depicted a typical family in various real-life settings discussing the potential impact of President Clinton's health care reform proposal. The advertising campaign, paid for by the health insurance industry, is credited as a major factor in the defeat of that proposal. The campaign had such lasting effects that, when the White House was negotiating the Affordable Care Act (or "Obamacare") in 2009, President Obama made a series of significant concessions to the industry in hopes they would stay quiet (and it worked). If these campaigns are well done and generate calls and emails to legislators, they can influence legislative decision-making. But elected officials have daunting schedules and will often never see the advertising. Unless the ads influence real activism—measured by the legislator's staff—they have little chance of influencing lawmakers.

4.10. You Are Competing with Everyone, Even Though You Don't Know It

When individuals participate in "lobby days" or "fly-ins" in Washington to advocate for a particular cause, attendees will often look at their issue and say, "This makes perfect sense! Who could oppose this idea?" The answer is, "Everyone!"

Every individual, constituency group, association, corporation, and nonprofit group "petitioning their government for a redress of grievances" is competing with you for the time, attention, and resources of a member of Congress and the U.S. government. Each legislator has a limited amount of energy and political capital to expend. Every year, the federal budget apportions a fixed amount of funds to be spent. Each year, the subcommittees of the House and Senate Appropriations Committees are allotted a set amount of money to spend on programs—an allotment that is nearly impossible to increase.

When a group meets with a legislator, that meeting is likely one of dozens the legislator is holding that week with similar groups (see Section 1.4 for a sample schedule of a member of Congress). As legislators and staff assess which proposal or appropriation to support, they are weighing it against hundreds of other requests for support. To stand out, you must distinguish your cause in some meaningful way, or a competing group will win the limited attention, resources, and support each legislator has to offer. (See Chapter 5 for strategies and tactics to help your issue rise above the rest.)

Part II
How to Influence a Legislator

The introduction of this book and Part I offered some lofty democratic ideals, beckoning readers to appreciate their unrealized strength as citizen-advocates and use it for some societal good. Part II is the application of that knowledge. All the passion in the world can't move a mountain without the right forklift and someone who knows how to use it.

This part includes overarching strategies for influencing legislators; how to make the most of face-to-face interactions with lawmakers and their staff; best practices for communications with Congress and state legislatures; how to leverage news media and research; and the strategic value of third-party voices.

Chapter 5
Strategies for Influencing Legislators

When I feel the heat, I see the light.

— Senator Everett Dirksen (R-Illinois, Senate Minority Leader, 1959–1969)

5.1 Get to Them BEFORE They Take a Stand

The first rule for influencing a legislator has to do with timing. If a member of Congress or a state legislator has already come to a decision, you will have a difficult time changing their position. Politicians learn early on in their careers that there is a huge price to pay for inconsistency. Reporters will crucify them as "flip-floppers" if they change a position. Therefore, once they take a position on an issue, they'll stick to it.

Rep. Mo Udall (D-Arizona) would tell a wonderful joke about politicians' and journalists' obsession with consistency. He would say, "If I killed my mother, the media wouldn't attack me for committing murder. They would point out that I advocated against matricide in my last campaign."

This doesn't mean it's impossible to turn a "no" into a "yes," and this book outlines ways to do just that. It merely suggests that it's *much* easier to turn an "undecided" into a "yes."

5.2. The Value of a Personal Story

It is impossible to overstate the importance of constituents' personal stories and the influence they have in the policy process. Legislators trying to determine the best policy outcome can wrestle with facts and figures until they are blurry-eyed. And yet, when they come face-to-face with an actual person whom the policy affects, it completely focuses their thinking. They no longer see data and reports associated with that policy; they see a person. And no matter the legislator's position on the issue—pro or con—she feels an obligation to the person: either to help him, or to adequately explain why she can't. "The most effective way to influence a lawmaker is for a constituent to talk to a legislator about how the policy will affect the person or a particular group," said one House Democrat.

If the story is powerful enough, and demonstrates some societal injustice or ill, it can actually be translated into legislation. "Megan's Law" requires law enforcement authorities to make information regarding sexual offenders available to the public. It was enacted because of the powerful story of a little girl who was abducted, raped, and killed. There is now a popular trend of naming bills after victims, such as "Heather's Law," "Rachel's Law," "Haley's Act," and the Amber Alert system.

On the lighter side, a constituent told a congressman about an unpleasant experience he had at the doctor's office. After being told to disrobe and put on a flimsy paper smock that didn't close in the back, the man was asked to sign papers related to his care without fully understanding their meaning. He felt quite uncomfortable and disadvantaged in the setting—and told his congressman so. This led the legislator to introduce a bill, "The No Private Contracts to Be Negotiated When the Patient is Buck Naked Act." Amusingly, this bill was introduced by Rep. Pete Stark (D-California), so it quickly became known as the "Stark Naked Act."

One House Democrat, who was a member of the powerful House Appropriations Committee, had a memorable experience which demonstrates the value of personal stories. "I went to a luncheon that was hosted by cancer centers in my state," he said. "Instead of having those guys in white coats doing their lobbying, they brought in patients—kids and their parents. They all got up and told their story. When it was done there wasn't a dry eye in the room. They gave us the human importance of those dollars we're being asked to appropriate. Every group needs to do that."

Mental Wellness and The Boston Marathon Bombing

Most Americans don't know where legislative ideas originate. They should be comforted to know the source: often, it's them! Many bills introduced in legislatures are prompted by a problem, need, or desire articulated by a legislator's constituent. The person will reach out to their lawmaker, explain the issue, and propose a solution. And sometimes, just like in the cartoon "I'm Just a Bill," the legislation becomes the law of the land.

Such a scenario played out after the tragedy of the Boston Marathon bombing. On April 15, 2014, Manya Chylinski was perched at the finish line of the iconic race. In a split second her life changed when two bombs exploded, killing three people and injuring hundreds more. Manya counted herself lucky, as she was not physically harmed. However, in the days and weeks that followed she was plagued with a variety of mental health issues. She experienced fear and anxiety, and was finally diagnosed with PTSD.

Unfortunately, she discovered that while the Federal Emergency Management Agency (FEMA) provided services for those physically harmed because of the bombing, individuals with mental health issues resulting from the disaster were given no assistance. She told this to her congresswoman, Rep. Ayanna Pressley (D-Massachusetts), who introduced bipartisan legislation to correct the problem. "When disaster strikes—whether it be a natural disaster or mass violence—survivors are often left grappling with lasting trauma that has devastating impacts on their mental health," Rep. Pressley said. And on December 22, 2022, the "Post-Disaster Mental Health Response Act" was signed into law by President Joe Biden. The law expands eligibility for FEMA's crisis counseling assistance, ensuring that people can access free crisis counseling and community care in the wake of traumatic events. "If we're talking about these things from day one, more people are going to know that help is available if they need it," Manya Chylinski said.

Sometimes the government works just like you learned in eighth grade social studies class!

5.3. How to Build Powerful Relationships with Legislators

The most effective advocates aren't those who suddenly become interested in an issue; they're the ones who demonstrate interest and expertise about a topic over time. Here are three tips for building a long-term relationship with a legislator.

1. Learn about your lawmaker.

Dale Carnegie taught us years ago that understanding someone else's problems and interests is the best way to "win friends and influence people." Politicians are people, too (contrary to what you might have read), and they're susceptible to the same types of influences. An advocate is going to be much more powerful if he starts a conversation by asking about a congresswoman's kid who just went to college, or mentioning that he saw her picture in the newspaper recently at a ribbon cutting. Before your meeting, learn what bills she's introduced, what issues she's spoken out on, and her recent accomplishments.

Start with the lawmaker's website. Their "media" or "press releases" or "issues" sections will contain their (albeit biased) perspective on how they view issues. Searching online for news stories will offer additional information. Some associations or nonprofits will produce annual or biannual "scorecards," assessing the lawmaker's support or opposition to the group's legislative agenda. Groups such as the National Rifle Association, League of Conservation Voters, Club for Growth, and Human Rights Campaign regularly examine the voting records of members of Congress and publish assessments. In many cases, these groups will send out a mass alert to Capitol Hill offices noting that an upcoming vote will be "scored," which usually results in legislators thinking twice about crossing the group.

2. Establish yourself as a helpful expert, and offer to be their researcher.

Lobbyists aren't successful at their job because they take members of Congress to lunch (that's now illegal). They're successful because they *know* the issues. The most valuable gift a lobbyist gives a member of Congress isn't a campaign contribution—it's a detailed analysis of how an issue affects the lawmaker's district or state. Some state association, nonprofit, and corporate leaders offer this data, but many do not. Identify and research how a particular issue affects the legislator's constituents, and she'll call *you* for advice. (More on this in Section 5.8.)

3. Communicate frequently.

Every congressional office knows those in-district advocates who stay on top of issues and don't hesitate to offer help or advice on how a legislator should vote. As a chief of staff in the House of Representatives, I knew weeks before a key vote affecting the environment that I would be called not only by Washington lobbyists, but by environmental activists back home. Keeping in regular contact with your legislators provides a valuable service to legislators and staff, and keeps them accountable to voters.

Resources on How to Track Your Lawmaker's Performance

Holding elected officials accountable to their constituents is a central tenet of American democracy. Yet, the most ubiquitous "tools" that are commonly available are the internet, social media, and mainstream media. With the fractured and often partisan slant of these sources, citizens are either purposely misled or woefully underserved by those services which claim to hold lawmakers accountable. Fortunately, some independent and reliable sources exist for helping the public understand the performance of the U.S. Congress and their individual lawmakers.

Center for Effective Lawmaking (thelawmakers.org). A joint venture of the University of Virginia and Vanderbilt University, the Center for Effective Lawmaking is one of the only resources which examines the legislative performance of Congress using objective criteria. Working with what's available in the public record, researchers have constructed an algorithm to measure legislative performance, such as introducing and passing legislation, offering amendments, and committee activity. While it does not measure the totality of a legislator's performance, it is the best tool to measure most of their legislative work.

Lugar Center's Bipartisan Index (thelugarcenter.org/ourwork-Bipartisan-Index.html). The Lugar Center was founded by former Senator Richard Lugar (R-Indiana), one of the most respected lawmakers in recent years by both Democrats and Republicans. It has developed a scorecard to examine whether members of Congress actively worked with colleagues on the other side of the aisle to develop and pass legislation.

Bipartisan Policy Center's Healthy Congress Index (bipartisanpolicy.org/congress). The Bipartisan Policy Center (BPC) created a Commission on Political Reform in 2013 to propose a series of institutional reforms designed to improve Congress. The Commission recommended changes to the congressional schedule, committee performance, and budgeting procedures. After every congressional session's two-year cycle, the BPC applies the recommendations' metrics to Congress as an institution to offer a performance index.

GovTrack (govtrack.us/congress/members). For the serious legislative wonks, a free service, GovTrack, was created by Joshua Tauberer, a self-described "software engineering manager and civic hacker." Prior to the congressional modernization efforts launched in the mid-2010s, GovTrack was one of the only publicly available tools to track individual pieces of legislation. Every two years GovTrack issues a "Report Card" on each lawmaker, assessing bills introduced, bills cosponsored, and committee activity.

Congressional Management Foundation Democracy Awards (congressfoundation.org/democracy-awards). Launched in 2018, the Congressional Management Foundation created an award for non-legislative performance of congressional offices. Sort of like the "Oscars for Congress," CMF assesses various categories and issues two awards (Democrat and Republican) in each category. Finalists are assessed by a committee of former members of Congress and staff to ensure objective and fair outcomes. (Transparency Note: I am the former CEO of CMF.)

Legis1 (legis1.com). Legis1 is a subscription-based online platform for tracking legislation, congressional staff, lobbyists, and a variety of activities related to the legislative process. The service includes a complete directory of members of Congress, staff, committees, and registered lobbyists. Alerts can be customized by topic, keyword, or legislation, allowing users to stay informed about issues important to them. (Transparency Note: Legis1 was created by the Sunwater Institute, the publisher of this book.)

Trade Associations and Nonprofits. For citizen-advocates passionate about individual causes or issues, the best sources for legislative tracking and accountability are often trade associations and nonprofit organizations. It's impossible for the average citizen to assume the role of a professional lobbyist, which usually requires advanced (and expensive) legislative tracking software. Fortunately, for nearly every issue there is a so-called "special interest group" that exists to advocate for a particular cause or group. By signing up to the group's e-newsletter, citizen-advocates will be able to review the group's legislative agenda and receive alerts to action when a vote, bill co-sponsorship, or letter writing campaign is relevant.

5.4. Leveraging Your Affiliations to Magnify Your Power

Politicians are really good at political math. They recognize that when a constituent is part of a broader group or network, any interaction with that individual could be communicated to the broader group—or that the constituent may represent the broader group's views. If they please this individual, they'll gain favor with a whole raft of other constituents.

For citizen-advocates, this means that participating in a group's advocacy efforts—such as those led by a trade association or nonprofit—amplifies your voice immensely. And elected officials will do the actual math, estimating how many constituents might be affiliated with that group. Said another way, the National Education Association with three million teachers has a greater voice in Congress than the National Court Reporters Association with 12,000 members.

There are a few organized groups that have a powerful voice in our democracy because of their reputation for organizing grassroots efforts in both legislative battles and elections. The American Association of Retired Persons (AARP), the National Rifle Association (NRA), and teachers' unions all represent the views of millions of Americans. Media critics often confuse this grassroots power with their fundraising capabilities, suggesting it's "special interest money" that influences lawmakers. The reality comes down to sheer numbers—people who share a common belief and are willing to put their vote behind that belief. You may disagree with their tactics and even their values, but democracies are supposed to be responsive to large numbers of voters. As one House Democrat from a southern state said, "[Interest group's] money is beside the point. They can mobilize and intensify a group of motivated constituents who can put the fear of God in members of Congress."

Other factors can influence lawmakers more than just the size of a group. Organizational chapters could have an important role in the community, or their local members could be big players in the district or state. For example, while the Rotary Club may not engage in advocacy efforts, their local membership could be the business leaders representing every corner of the local economy. Or the lawmaker or someone he knows could have a personal connection to the group or cause.

To amplify your voice, consider getting involved with organizations in one of these ways:

- Sign up for their advocacy e-newsletter. Nearly every national or state nonprofit or trade association sends out regular updates on issues or legislation important to the group. Subscribing to these e-newsletters is the best way to stay on top of issues you care about.

- Opt-in to receive "Action Alerts." Organizations understand that mobilizing thousands of constituents to take action is a key strategy for influencing lawmakers, especially those who are undecided on an issue. In the email message sent by the group you'll see a link to a section of the group's website which allows you to enter your local address and modify your message to lawmakers. With local address information, the website will display your elected officials and who will receive this message. This grassroots software, created in the late 1990s, is now ubiquitous among trade associations and nonprofits. These alerts often respond to fast-moving developments, like quick and unexpected committee votes, so timing is often crucial. Follow the instructions exactly and localize and personalize the top of the message. Add an anecdote or note how many members of your organization live in the lawmaker's district or state.

- Consider donating to the group's political action committee (PAC). As noted in Section 4.7, campaign contributions do not typically determine legislative outcomes—but they are noticed by the candidate, and sometimes can lead to more access to the lawmaker.

Research on people who join associations and nonprofits shows they are more likely to write to a lawmaker about an issue, more likely to vote, more likely to sign a petition, and more likely to participate in political campaigns. Politicians know this, and by joining others in exercising your constitutional right to "petition the government for a redress of grievances," your chances of swaying the lawmaker greatly increase.

Chart 3 Survey of Congressional Staff

If your Member/Senator has not already arrived at a firm decision on an issue, how much influence might the following advocacy strategies directed to your office have on their decision?

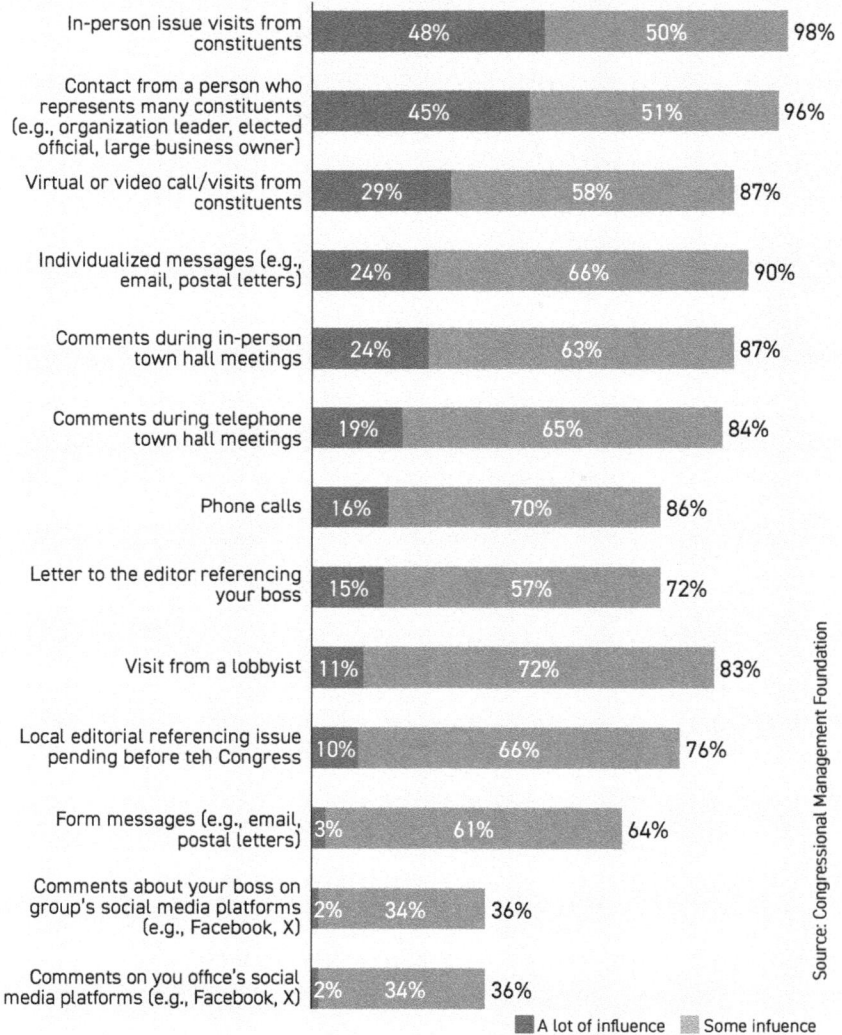

Strategy	A lot of influence	Some influence	Total
In-person issue visits from constituents	48%	50%	98%
Contact from a person who represents many constituents (e.g., organization leader, elected official, large business owner)	45%	51%	96%
Virtual or video call/visits from constituents	29%	58%	87%
Individualized messages (e.g., email, postal letters)	24%	66%	90%
Comments during in-person town hall meetings	24%	63%	87%
Comments during telephone town hall meetings	19%	65%	84%
Phone calls	16%	70%	86%
Letter to the editor referencing your boss	15%	57%	72%
Visit from a lobbyist	11%	72%	83%
Local editorial referencing issue pending before teh Congress	10%	66%	76%
Form messages (e.g., email, postal letters)	3%	61%	64%
Comments about your boss on group's social media platforms (e.g., Facebook, X)	2%	34%	36%
Comments on you office's social media platforms (e.g., Facebook, X)	2%	34%	36%

A lot of influence   Some infuence

Source: Congressional Management Foundation

5.5. How to Influence Legislators Who Don't Represent You

Citizen-advocates often ask, "How do I influence a legislator who doesn't represent my district?" The answer is, "It's complicated." The Founders gave us a representative democracy—a republic. We elect individuals to represent our interests in Washington and state capitals. If they don't do that well, our only option is to vote them out of office.

One way to influence someone who you don't have an opportunity to vote for is to expand your economic and political footprint. Identify where you might have interests and use that leverage to influence legislators. A business owner may live in District 1 but operates her business in District 2. She is perfectly within her rights as a citizen to send an email to the District 2 congressman with the opening, "I run a flower shop in your district and employ 10 people in your town." You may also play some representational role in an association or group. The leader of the state teachers' association did not live in the district that a congressman represented, but the congressman always made time to meet with him because he spoke for 3,000 teachers in his district.

Another way to influence a legislator who doesn't represent you is to get *your* representative to do it for you. One of the fun secrets of legislatures is the unexpected friendships that blossom between chambers and parties. Two lawmakers from opposite parties representing the same midwestern state became close friends because one of them was going through a nasty divorce—something the other had also gone through. Plus, because of the congressional schedule, the lawmakers were often booked on the same flight and sat next to each other. (This had the added benefit of preventing one or two constituents from monopolizing the legislators' time on a two-hour flight.)

Legislators bond in a variety of ways. They may have come from the same profession or serve on the same committees. And many women lawmakers have a special bond in legislatures, especially in the U.S. Senate. In part it's due to their shared experiences of putting up with discrimination and misogyny as they entered politics. Veterans who serve in Congress also share the common connection of serving in the military. If you want to connect with a lawmaker from a district far from you, just ask your lawmaker if they know that person. Your best advocacy ally may have friends in high places.

5.6. How to Influence Congressional Committee Staff

Staff who work for congressional committees are hard to influence, somewhat reclusive, and among the most powerful people in Washington. Each congressional committee chairman recruits a team of people to write the bills that become law. These individuals are usually experts in their field, with formidable intellects and impeccable academic and professional credentials.

Influencing this cadre is the most difficult part of the advocacy process. Yet, you have a couple of options to connect with committee staff. One entrée to this group is possible through a professional lobbyist. Your nonprofit group or trade association probably employs someone who is hired to build relationships with committee staff. Your best (and maybe only) way to access this person is through your lobbyist. If your story is representative of a particular governmental issue or problem, the person actually drafting legislation to address the problem will want to hear about it. Petition your group to set up a call or meeting between you and a committee staffer, and make sure your story is heard.

Some advocates lament that they can't influence congressional committees if they are not represented by a member of the committee. Yet this is the byproduct of a representative democracy. Citizens can most easily influence those elected officials they have a connection to. If you have no connection to a legislator—even though they may sit on a committee especially relevant to your cause—your job, as an advocate, is to build or identify a connection. Perhaps a friend in a neighboring district is represented by someone on the committee. Or you belong to a trade association or nonprofit with a broad membership network. If you cold-call a congressional committee, the assistant will ask you for your home address and quickly transfer you to the office of your member of Congress. Only through some tangible political link can an interested party influence a congressional committee.

5.7. Creating a Network and Mobilizing Assets

A more advanced advocacy strategy is to include others in your effort. Everyone has a "network," although they may not think of it that way. It may include friends, family, professional acquaintances, or people who have a connection to an organization you belong to. Recruiting others to join your cause amplifies your voice from one to many, and is much more likely to get the attention of lawmakers. A chorus of voices all singing from the same hymnal make a powerful statement to an elected official.

If you're part of a nonprofit organization, the first logical candidates are your board of directors. You could also consider major donors or even regular volunteers. One of them could have a prior relationship with an elected official who can help move your issue forward. In your professional world, you may have a work colleague who is in the same club or belongs to the same place of worship as a representative. It's perfectly ok to ask for their help, politely inquiring if they're interested in supporting your cause.

When recruiting fellow advocates, consider the variety of assets they bring to your effort. What are their skill sets? What kinds of relationships do they have with elected officials? And how much are they trusted by those officials on this issue?

It's also wise to look beyond the "usual suspects." A few years ago, a nonprofit leader was conducting a regular board meeting not long after an election had changed the majority in her state assembly. She was bemoaning that the group had lost a great champion who no longer chaired a key committee, and didn't know the new chairman. The newest and youngest member of the board raised her hand. The young woman had been recruited to the board for her communications skills to improve the nonprofit's social media presence. "Maybe I can help," she said. Every head turned in disbelief. How could this twenty-something know a powerful chairman in the legislature? "Do you think he would take a meeting if you asked?" the nonprofit leader asked. "He better," the young woman replied. "He came to my wedding."

If you don't ask you won't know if you have gold in your network. Simple inquiries can transform a single voice into a chorus—one strong enough to shift the course of legislation.

5.8. How to Map Your Economic and Political Footprint

Every citizen has an economic and political footprint that connects them to government. The taxes you pay, employees you hire, clubs you belong to—anything that demonstrates your power as a citizen—goes into the equation. Some citizens have a greater economic and political footprint than others, such as union leaders, state association presidents, or CEOs of large companies. These individuals can claim to be the voice of others and command greater attention from elected officials. However, if you genuinely consider the breadth and depth of your world, you'd be surprised at how powerful you would seem to a politician.

Start by considering your home and work. If you live in one congressional district and work in another, you'll instantly find yourself represented by two members of Congress. "But don't legislators only represent constituents who can vote for them?" Yes, technically that is correct. However, politicians are savvy enough to know that you talk to coworkers. If he messes up, you'll end up talking trash about him next time you're at the water cooler.

Now consider every organization you belong to or are affiliated with. This includes professional associations, clubs, school groups, alumni chapters, and even organizations you give charitable donations to. Every one of these connections gives you an opportunity to expand your political footprint. When you start your letter to a congresswoman with, "I'm a member of [insert well known group here]," the legislator doesn't see a single individual, she sees an entire group, and you as its representative voice.

Finally, when all the affiliations are burned away, you might be surprised to learn what category of citizens start out with a very large political footprint: college students. The organizer of a graduate student group conducting their first lobby day on Capitol Hill asked, "Should we try to set up meetings with legislators who represent our home districts, or where we go to school?" The correct answer is: "Both!" U.S. election laws allow college students to register to vote *either* where they reside or where they go to school. As a result, elected officials don't *know* which district or state this young person might vote in—and will treat them as a potential voter in both.

Advocacy Success Story: Alzheimer's Association

Some advocacy efforts in Washington stem from the government relations and grassroots teams of a national trade association or nonprofit identifying a bill or topic they wish to champion on behalf of their stakeholders. Other issues are more organic, emerging from a societal need that only the government can address. Such is the case with Alzheimer's disease and other dementia.

About one in nine Americans over the age of 65 has Alzheimer's or dementia. One estimate is that 40 percent of our population will eventually either get the fatal disease or care for someone who will. The cost of care for people living with Alzheimer's in 2021 was $450 billion in the U.S., and without a cure that cost will balloon to $3.5 trillion by 2060.

There are so many advocacy success stories that happen every year at the federal, state, and local government level. But because they may only have a small group of stakeholders (compared to the U.S. population), few outside of that group know of the successes. Happily, one successful group is the Alzheimer's Association, the leading voluntary health organization in Alzheimer's care, support, and research.

Because of the immense toll that these diseases inflict on America, the Alzheimer's Association had a massive challenge. Effective and meaningful change to government policy would entail massive financial investments, require dozens of federal agencies to coordinate research, and involve nearly every member of Congress. To address this challenge, they created the Alzheimer's Ambassador program in 2010. According to their website, Ambassadors are grassroots volunteers who commit to serve for a renewable one-year term as the main point of in-district contact for a specific member of Congress. And Alzheimer's Congressional Team (ACT) members bring their own unique stories, relationships and skills to complement the work of an Ambassador. Ambassadors and ACT members develop trusted relationships with their assigned congressional office and draw upon proven techniques through the support of Association staff.

By developing relationships and telling personal stories, the Alzheimer's Association has achieved more legislative success than any other patient advocacy group in the last two decades. In 2011, the group facilitated the passage of the National Alzheimer's Project Act (NAPA), which consolidated the federal government's disjointed efforts—previously spread across multiple federal agencies—and put the Department of Health and Human Services in charge of a coordinated effort. Over the next ten years, federal investment in Alzheimer's and dementia research increased by 700 percent.

One reason for this success is Ambassadors like Suzanne Wronsky of Potomac, Maryland. Suzanne's passion for the cause came from the same tragic source as many patient advocates: her mother developed dementia and eventually died of Alzheimer's. "I was nervous about this and I hadn't really given much thought to engaging with my elected officials before that point—it just wasn't something that was in my wheelhouse," Suzanne said in an interview.

At first, she started small. "We did legislative breakfasts and things like that where we had elected officials come to us in a very informal setting," she said. "I remember my first speech and my hands shaking with the paper and reading word for word what I had written down. I'm thinking it is too long and of course I'm crying during the talk," she said.

Suzanne continued to increase her involvement with the Alzheimer's movement, including meeting with her elected officials in Congress. "When I hear about the do-nothing Congress, I just get a prickly feeling because it's not my experience in my interactions with elected officials," she said. "I just think too many regular citizens don't realize what they can do and choose not to be involved."

Suzanne became so confident—and a "go-to" person on the topic—that at one point, when her local congressman wanted to give a speech on the floor about Alzheimer's, his district director called her for information about the disease. He wanted to tell her story on the floor of the U.S. House of Representatives.

"Everybody's story is so valuable and important," Suzanne said. "I just encourage folks to tell their story and know that they have the right to tell it."

5.9. How NOT to Advocate

Soon after Donald Trump's inauguration as president in 2017, House Republicans saw a surge in attendance at their local town hall meetings—and not in a good way. Constituents were furious with both Trump's tone and policies. In Green Bay, Wisconsin, a man came to his congressman's town hall meeting with a home-made sign which read, "I DIDN'T COME HERE TO LISTEN TO YOU… I CAME HERE TO YELL!!!!"

Public protests are a time-honored and valuable part of the mosaic of American democracy. The nonviolent protests of the Civil Rights era galvanized support for passing civil rights legislation. The massive protests against the Vietnam War demonstrated public opposition to the war. Even in the nation's founding days, the 1773 Boston Tea Party—protesting taxation without representation—tied the concept of protest to the very essence of our rights as citizens.

However, the boundary between protest and intimidation of elected officials and election workers has become blurry in recent years. Two members of Congress, Representatives Gabby Giffords and Steve Scalise, were shot by irate individuals. A member of the U.S. House resigned *midterm* in 2023, hinting that threats against his family were a factor in his decision. And the U.S. Capitol Police reports that the number of death threats against members of Congress increased by 500 to 1,000 percent between 2017 and 2021.

For many Americans, the issues and challenges facing our democracy seem existential, allowing them to justify behavior that would have been unthinkable in another era. But for elected officials, the transition from protest to intimidation represents a different kind of existential threat: it's personal.

Sometimes the de-evolution of advocacy stems from simple over-enthusiasm. But when a group crosses a line with an elected official or their staffer, it can result in a lifetime ban from future advocacy with that office. A few years ago, a business group lobbying a Senate office was meeting with the senator's chief of staff regarding a piece of pending legislation. The group wanted the senator to cosponsor the bill. The staff member noted that the senator would participate in a committee hearing in a few weeks on the legislation and wanted to decide after the hearing whether to cosponsor it—an eminently reasonable position for an elected official to take. But that wasn't good enough for the business group. They distributed the chief of staff's *direct desk number*, which resulted in him being bombarded with hundreds of calls and unable to use his office phone for weeks. Not only did the senator not cosponsor the bill (in part due to his fury at the business group for targeting his senior staff member), but the group also never met with that senior staffer again.

Public protests, rallies, email campaigns—every elected official deems these reasonable and a bedrock American right. But mobs showing up at a lawmaker's or judge's home, hurling disgusting insults at spouses and children, and leaving voicemails threatening violence against a member of Congress are beyond the pale. No bill, no issue, no cause can justify this behavior. When considering your strategies, realize that the person you're advocating before *is a person*. They have feelings and families just like you do and will recoil against an entire group of advocates if just one of them crosses the line from protest to something worse.

5.10. Building Relationships with Freshman Legislators

In January 2023, at the start of the 118th Congress, more than half of the members of the House of Representatives waiting to be sworn in had four years of congressional experience or less. Often, term limits supporters claim that the problem with our democracy is that there is not enough turnover in our national legislature. Guess what? We have term limits in America—they're called "elections," and the voters seem to be doing a pretty good job of cycling out the dead wood in our democracy. For citizen-advocates, this means you frequently have a fresh crop of elected officials just waiting for their constituents to reach out.

New lawmakers, often called "freshmen," present a different set of opportunities and challenges for citizen-advocates. The opportunity is that most freshmen legislators have not yet taken firm positions on most of the issues they'll consider. It is possible that they made a commitment on the campaign trail or voted on the issue as a state or local official. But because they have no legislative history in this legislature they're looking for new ideas. "A lot of our initial legislative ideas came from constituents, and it resulted in some of the most successful bills," said a House communications director working for a first-term member of Congress.

The challenge, especially for new members of the U.S. House and Senate, is that it takes a few months for legislators and their staff to set up the organizational apparatus needed to process constituent communications and conduct professional outreach to local groups. Setting up a new congressional office is like launching a new small business. While congressional offices are expected to be up and running on Swearing-In Day—January 3—they are typically not fully staffed on that day and may not even have a district office in which to hold meetings.

Smart advocates realize that building relationships with elected officials early in their tenure in office can translate into lifelong champions. Here are some tips for connecting with freshmen lawmakers.

Send Congratulations Notes. Every newly elected official loves seeing congratulatory notes on their electoral victory—even if you don't belong to an organization. If you do have a connection with a local, state, or national organization, be sure to note it in your email or letter, and suggest you plan to follow up with a request for a visit after they are sworn in. This puts you on their radar early, making the future visit more memorable.

Meet in the District. Offices in Washington and state capitals may take time to fully set up. Immediately after swearing-in, lawmakers and their staff are likely still getting used to their new environment and grappling with the furious pace of a legislative session. Freshmen lawmakers know the district and are more comfortable meeting with constituents on their home turf. Even if you don't have office space, find a third-party space to meet—an office building or a coffee shop, or request a meeting at the legislator's district or state office. There will be fewer time constraints and potential interruptions compared to state or federal meetings in the capital city.

Set Up Events. New lawmakers and their staff are overwhelmed in their first few weeks and months on the job. This is an opportunity for citizen-advocates to create meaningful interactive events and meetings. Since new staff may have never staged an event with their lawmaker, groups and citizens who provide a ready-made venue for a "photo op" and an engaged audience for dialogue are welcomed. You're basically giving these freshmen legislators a big fat political gift wrapped up in a bow. (See Section 6.1 for a how-to guide in requesting and setting up a meeting or event with a lawmaker.)

Get to Know Senior Staff. Nearly every state lawmaker and all members of Congress have staff. Some may have known the legislator for years; others may have worked on the campaign or are new to the team. As noted in Section 6.7, building relationships with a legislator's staff is a key ingredient for successful advocacy. Your goal is to quickly establish yourself as a trusted expert on your topic. The staffer may not be as knowledgeable about the topic as you are, and your local perspective is valuable data to that staffer and elected official.

Use Social Media. Nearly every legislator has a communications budget to engage with their constituents. Freshman members of the U.S. House can sometimes spend $250,000 annually on e-newsletters, social media ads, and telephone town hall meetings. However, the tools and procedures for creating and delivering that content is not yet ready in the first few months in office. Instead, social media is one of the only tools they have to interact with large numbers of their constituents. So, savvy advocates should jump into X, Facebook, Instagram, and the other platforms du jour to connect with new lawmakers. The degree to which these politicians use social media varies wildly based on the individual's technical comfort level and interests. But if they are active in social media, it means they're watching what people say about them. Take advantage of the social media-addicted lawmaker and push content to them or respond to their feed. And as noted in Section 7.4, any photo captured of you, your colleagues, and the lawmaker or their staff should be posted in your social media accounts and sent to the legislator's staff. If they repost your content, you're not just influencing the lawmaker but all her followers as well.

Chapter 6
Face-to-Face Meetings

People don't care how much you know until they know how much you care.
— **Robert B. Cialdini**

As noted in research cited throughout this book, state and federal lawmakers say nothing replaces face-to-face contact with constituents. Every legislator—at the local, state, and federal level—has a system and set of procedures for managing meetings with constituents. Here are some tips for excelling at this activity.

6.1. Scheduling a Meeting with a Legislator

The system that a legislator uses for managing meetings with constituents will vary depending on what level of government you're reaching out to. If you're contacting a member of the New Hampshire House of Representatives, where each member represents about 3,300 people, you'll likely deal directly with the legislator through email and phone. If you're goal is to meet with a member of Congress, you'll likely fill out a form requesting a meeting. For whatever method you pursue, it is important that you follow their prescribed instructions for a meeting request, lest you get shoved aside for failing to adhere to their protocols. Here are some general guidelines for setting up a meeting with a lawmaker.

First, visit their website and see if there is any guidance on requesting a meeting. Nearly every member of Congress has a scheduling request form on their website to fill out. Provide as much information as you can on the webform, including:

1. Names of constituents seeking a meeting;

2. The topic or issue you wish to discuss;

3. Any organization you're connected to which has an interest in the issue;

4. Potential dates for the meeting;

5. Possible locations for the meeting; and

6. Contact information (email and cell phone numbers).

When suggesting dates/times for the meeting, it is best to be as flexible as possible. Constituents who propose exact times and dates can get a quick "no" because the lawmaker may be booked during that time. If you are hoping to meet with a member of Congress in their state office, it's wise to consult the House and Senate annual calendar (easily accessible through a Google search) so you can identify the recesses/district work periods when the legislator is back home.

When making the request, try to tie the meeting to something specific: a bill pending in the legislature, an issue related to their committee work, or a concern affecting their district. Politicians are always doing the political math when interacting with constituents who have an opinion or interest in an issue. In your meeting request, do the math for them and let them know the issue could affect many constituents. If you have allies from various groups who also want to attend, include that information. If the lawmaker can make multiple groups happy with one meeting, they'll gladly double up.

You may not get an instant email back acknowledging the request. If you have not heard back in two weeks, it's best to follow up with the office. Their silence may be the result of the lawmaker or staff being overwhelmed, or perhaps there is an administrative error in processing the request. Know that the lawmaker and their staff have just as much interest as you do in scheduling and conducting a successful meeting. The easier you make it for them to say "yes" to the request, the more likely you are to have a good interaction.

How to Turn a Chance Meeting into a Legislative Victory

So, you're in the supermarket, waiting in line, and you notice the person behind you is none other than your member of Congress. Should you press them with your favorite issue and intrude on what is clearly their "personal time"? The answer is, "HELL, YES!" Legislators expect that as public figures they will be subject to all degrees of influence when they are in public. A polite and respectful request is not only expected, but is often welcome, as legislators use these encounters as yet another barometer of public opinion.

One U.S. senator loved going to the supermarket to shop because she interacted with so many constituents over an hour or two. (She also learned to go to the frozen food section last, because if she went there first, the ice cream would melt before she got to the checkout line due to all the conversations along the way with constituents.)

Another member of Congress told me that while he was coaching first base for his son's Little League team, a mother on the opposing team took the opportunity to lecture him on U.S. foreign policy. (This is almost a perfect advocacy anecdote, because the lawmaker was stuck coaching first base until the home team had three outs!)

If you've got an opportunity for a one-on-one, grab it—then herald the interaction on your organization's blog or website. One senator said it this way: "When I'm at home and I've had individual citizens come tell me about a problem, and then I continue to hear about it, I do something about it. It's the repetitiveness of it. I go home and get the temperature of things. I say to people, don't hesitate to mention something to an elected official."

6.2. Tips for Meeting with Legislators and Staff

When in Washington, members of the U.S. House of Representatives typically meet with 5–8 groups of constituents each day—and their staff may meet with another 20. Each group is petitioning the legislator or staffer with a specific ask: to cosponsor legislation, vote "yea" or "nay" on an upcoming bill, or request an earmark (now called "Community Project Funding") from the House or Senate Appropriations Committee. These sessions tend to last 10–20 minutes and involve 2–20 constituents. As Chart 4 (Section 6.3) notes, they are the most influential tool in any advocate's toolkit. Here are 10 tips for maximizing the potential for success when meeting with a legislator in Washington or a state capital.

1. Know who you're talking to. It's important to conduct research on the legislator you plan to meet with. Does he have some connection to your issue, either through background or current committee assignments? What recent legislative or press activity has he engaged in? What did his parents do for a living? Any of these answers could potentially open the door to his support. For example, a recently elected member of the U.S. House of Representatives has an odd connection to the radio broadcasting industry: her grandmother was one of the first female radio reporters in the country. When she meets with broadcasters, she has a preexisting connection to their industry. Your goal is to find that connection.

2. Know your issue. A U.S. senator once said there are two types of people she meets with: people who come prepared to meetings and people who don't. "If they come prepared, I listen to them. If they don't, they listen to me. The first group has much more influence," she said. Some groups think their strength in numbers will carry the day, or that consistently contributing to the legislator's campaign is all that's required. But neither of those components trumps a thoughtful constituent with command of the facts. "There are groups that come in with all the facts, and they're great," said a Senate state director. "Others come with just the soundbites they pick up on Twitter, and then you can't really have a conversation. They will swear what they tell you is factual, but then they can't speak on that topic beyond the 120 characters that they read."

3. Prepare a personal story. As noted earlier, personal stories are often more persuasive than raw facts. If you go in a group, determine before the meeting who's got the best story. A pro-life Republican recounted how he bucked his party and decided to support federal funding for stem-cell research. He said families who had children with juvenile diabetes visited him during a national group's advocacy day. One teenager talked about his life, how he coped with the disease, and his hope that the research could someday lead to a cure. "It was just one of those meetings that had a huge impact," the congressman said.

4. Refine your presentation. You might have 15 minutes with a legislator or staffer to make your pitch. Should you deliver one of the most important speeches of your life unrehearsed? Take half an hour the day before your meeting and practice your presentation. Place the best arguments first. Say it aloud, in front of the mirror, or a spouse, or your cat. Do everything to ensure that a weak presentation will not diminish your good ideas.

5. Don't arrive too early. Office space on Capitol Hill is cramped. I'm amused when television shows portray meetings with congressional staff in huge, mahogany-lined rooms, with waiters serving coffee from silver carafes. I think, "That must be the other Congress where I didn't work." Because of the lack of space, offices literally cannot accommodate early arrivals. House offices may have one or two chairs—maybe a couch if they're lucky. Roam the halls, fix your hair, get some coffee, but don't arrive more than five minutes before the meeting.

6. Deliver your message in the first 10 minutes—unless you're in the state office. Small talk and rapport-building are important and necessary, but get down to business quickly. Most constituent meetings with legislators in Washington last 15 minutes. Votes, important phone calls, and other distractions often interrupt meetings. After you've chatted about kids and sports, let her know why you're there. The exception to this rule is if you're meeting in a lawmaker's district office. As noted in Section 6.4, meetings in the state last longer, usually at least 30 minutes, so you have time for a more casual approach.

7. Always have a specific ask. The most crucial role of advocacy in our democratic process is to hold elected officials accountable. Advocates should have specific requests—usually with a "yes/no" option—to create a metric that the legislator can be measured by. The most common request is for a vote or a bill co-sponsorship. Yet it could be asking them to write a letter to a federal agency or give a speech in a committee meeting. The key is to be very clear. In 2005, Judge John Roberts was nominated to be Chief Justice of the Supreme Court. One national group launched an email campaign urging supporters to send messages asking senators to "Ask tough questions of Judge Roberts." How do you hold a senator accountable to a request like that? Do you really think a senator was going to reply to that message with, "Actually, I favor easy questions for Supreme Court nominees, like their favorite movie or baseball team." How can you hold them accountable if you don't have anything specific to hold them accountable to?

8. Never go off-message. At the start of a meeting between a well-known business group and a senator, the leader of the group was expected to discuss the tax issue that had brought him and ten other businessmen to Washington. The topic of the meeting was supposed to be a federal regulation under consideration that would cost this industry hundreds of millions of dollars. Instead, one of the participants began the conversation by saying, "Our lobbyist wants us to tell you about this federal regulation which supposedly is vital to our industry… but instead I want to talk to you about abortion." Consistency in message between professional-advocates (lobbyists) and citizen-advocates is essential to any successful advocacy efforts. The impulse to "freelance" usually ends in disaster. Interest groups, associations, and companies keep full time staff in Washington and state capitals for a reason—to identify those issues most relevant to the group and guide supporters with the correct message. Activists who don't follow their professional staff's advice may feel good about the liberating experience, but they're acting against their own interests. You might find yourself in a meeting with a politician you disagree with. You have to put those personal feelings in a parking lot, and pledge to write them an email later. If you and your group are meeting with lawmakers on a topic agreed upon in advance, it's important to stick to the script.

9. Provide feedback to professional lobbyists. One quality that distinguishes strong advocacy efforts from weak ones is close coordination between grassroots advocates and professional-advocates. After meeting with a legislator or staff it is *essential* that supporters provide feedback on the outcome of the meeting. When I was a chief of staff for a member of the House, a trade association lobbyist dropped by and asked this: "I understand one of our members ran into your boss at the grocery store and asked him to cosponsor our bill. We haven't heard back from you about this request—what should I tell your constituent?" I froze. That kind of coordination between a professional-advocate and citizen-advocate is rare. We prioritized that question and got an answer back to the lobbyist and the constituent. More importantly, every *future* request from the lobbyist or one of her members in our district became a top priority for the office.

10. Follow up within two weeks. When public officials are posed a specific question or given a clear request, they sometimes reply, "I'll look into it and get back to you." Either because of the crush of work or political necessity, sometimes they won't get back to you. The responsibility falls on the grassroots supporter to follow up. In most cases, the legislator or staff has accidentally let the issue or question fall through the cracks, so a follow-up call is needed. It also says to the official, "I'm not going away until you answer this question." One House chief of staff was asked, "Who do you listen to?" He replied, "I hate to admit it, but we listen to the squeaky wheels who won't go away." This doesn't mean calling the office daily demanding an answer to your question. But persistently and politely asking for a resolution is your right as a citizen. (More on the research behind the value of follow-ups in Chart 5, Section 6.9.)

Finally, appreciate that a legislator may be in a tough spot. Most constituents—and even some lobbyists—fail to understand that a lawmaker may genuinely want to please two groups of constituents who are pitted against one another. The wise citizen-petitioner will empathize with the struggling politician, perhaps even gaining his trust. "I particularly admire someone who's able to articulate the opposing argument, that can give a good faith account of the other side," said one House Democrat. "They seem to understand my situation, and I respect that."

6.3. Tips for Virtual Meetings with Lawmakers and Staff

Congress and state legislatures—like everyone else—went 100 percent virtual in March of 2020 with the onset of the COVID-19 pandemic. Over time, members of Congress and their staffs came to see new benefits in virtual meetings. They could connect easily with constituents and stakeholders; the economic and logistical barriers of traveling to Washington or the state capital were eliminated; and large and diverse gatherings could be convened on short notice.

Some lessons have emerged about what to do and what not to do in virtual meetings with lawmakers.

Here are some "DO's."

DO the same prep work you would for an in-person meeting. Just because you're dialing in from your kitchen table in your sweatpants doesn't mean you should be undisciplined about the encounter. Technology and setting may be different, but your advocacy goals are not.

DO choreograph the session like a stage production. Congressional staff have privately groused about poorly organized virtual meetings. Whether as an organizer or participant, it's important to have a clean implementation of the event. Consider who will deliver the main content, who will add a personal story, and who will make the "ask" of the lawmaker or staffer.

DO add some interesting visuals. While you can bring photographs and maps to an in-person meeting, adding them to a virtual meeting makes them "pop out" to participants. You don't need a multi-page PowerPoint presentation—but a few graphs or other visuals will make the meeting more memorable for the legislator.

DO get the technical stuff right. This interaction could be very important to you and others who support your cause. It would be tragic if you left a bad impression because someone hadn't tested their Zoom account before the meeting. A short "dress rehearsal" with your friends might be a wise precaution.

Here are some "DON'Ts."

DON'T dictate the technology platform. Some legislatures use their own virtual meeting platforms. Others have security settings which may not sync with your preferred software. Always ask the lawmaker's staff whether they want to host the meeting and what platform they prefer.

DON'T introduce any surprises. Politicians and their staffs hate surprises. Adding an unexpected speaker or topic will leave bad feelings and will work against your cause.

DON'T complain if they won't turn on their camera. Congressional staff are especially lazy when it comes to virtual meetings, sometimes multi-tasking instead of focusing on the constituent in the meeting. Regrettably, you must accept this virtual snub and deliver your content professionally and courteously.

Chart 4 Survey of Congressional Staff

How frequently do you experience the following in constituent meetings?

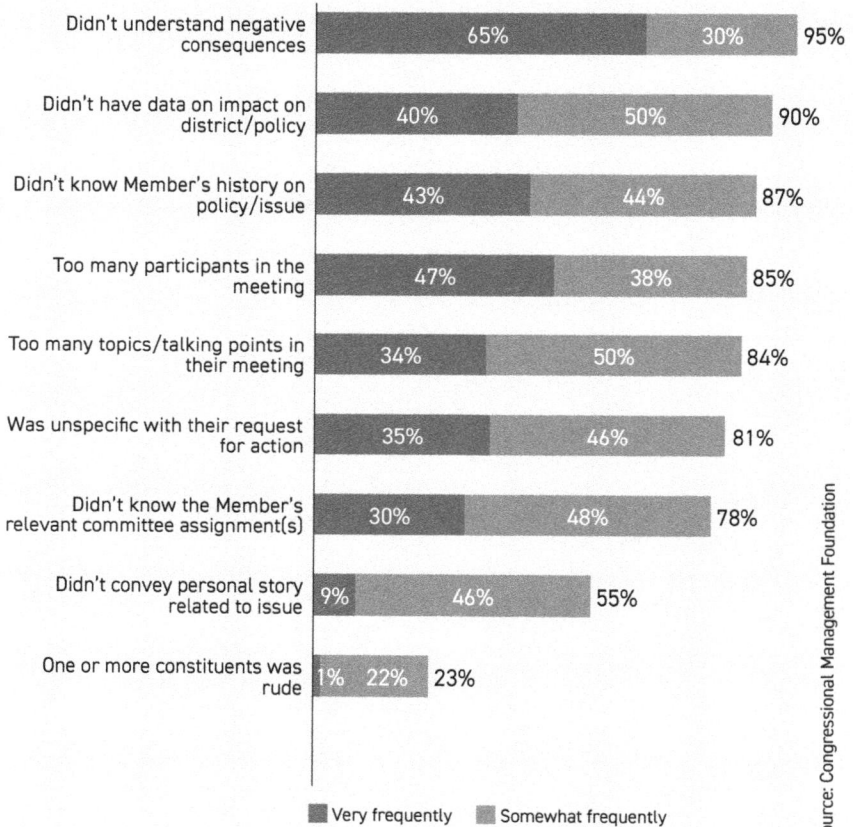

Category	Very frequently	Somewhat frequently	Total
Didn't understand negative consequences	65%	30%	95%
Didn't have data on impact on district/policy	40%	50%	90%
Didn't know Member's history on policy/issue	43%	44%	87%
Too many participants in the meeting	47%	38%	85%
Too many topics/talking points in their meeting	34%	50%	84%
Was unspecific with their request for action	35%	46%	81%
Didn't know the Member's relevant committee assignment(s)	30%	48%	78%
Didn't convey personal story related to issue	9%	46%	55%
One or more constituents was rude	1%	22%	23%

■ Very frequently   ■ Somewhat frequently

Source: Congressional Management Foundation

6.4 Strategies for In-State Advocacy

Many people associate advocacy with Washington and believe that citizen-advocates must travel to our nation's capital to meet with their lawmaker.

Yet a significant amount of constituent interaction does not involve meeting in and around a legislature. Members of Congress and state legislators often prefer meeting their constituents closer to home. They view these meetings as opportunities to learn first-hand about an issue, bill, or a regulation that affects their neighbors.

Here are some strategies citizens can employ back home.

In-State Meetings

Lawmakers often prefer to meet with constituents in their local offices for a few reasons. First, away from the hectic pace of a legislative session, these meetings usually are conducted without interruption and can last longer—at least 30 minutes. District and state offices are often more spacious, so they can accommodate more constituents in the meeting. And the advocates can also build relationships with the local staff, who can become invaluable champions for their cause. Smart citizen-advocates will build relationships with the state staff as well as the Washington staff. The turnover rate for U.S. House legislative assistants is about two years, whereas the House district directors often stay in their jobs ten years or more. In-state meetings, then, are not just valuable for connecting with a member of Congress—they're a great opportunity to make a friend on their staff. (To learn the process for requesting an in-state meeting with a legislator, see Section 6.1.)

Office Hours

Many lawmakers schedule regular times in the community to take "walk-in" visits with constituents. "Congress at Your Corner" might feature a member of the U.S. House parked outside of a grocery store with a couple of chairs and a folding table. It was at such an event in 2011 when a mentally unstable man approached Congresswoman Gabby Giffords (D-AZ), shooting her and killing six others. Even with the potential dangers, legislators still host these gatherings. Rep. Barry Moore (R-Alabama) hosts "Breakfast with Barry," or "BBQ with Barry," mixing fun names with food in his constituent interactions. To learn whether your lawmakers hold these kinds of events, simply phone their local office.

Site Visits

Politicians love meeting with their constituents at locations throughout the state and district. They view these hands-on events as rich opportunities to get their own perspective on an issue or learn more about a group. Additionally, they offer great visuals, making them wonderful for photo opportunities and media stories. It also is a chance to meet with many constituents, demonstrating a connection to a group of employees, association members, or nonprofit volunteers. (For a complete checklist of tasks for setting up an event with a local elected official, see Section 6.9.)

Finally, citizen-advocates should appreciate that in-state staff serve dual roles: they represent their member of Congress and act as ombudsmen/ customer service agents for the constituent. To the staffer, it doesn't matter what your politics are. "In the state, doesn't matter if you're a Democrat, Republican, Independent, Communist, or Socialist—we're apolitical," said one U.S. Senate state director.

The same Republican state director described a situation in 2017 when protesters against the policies of President Donald Trump would show up at their offices every Tuesday. "We called them the Trump Tuesday Crowd," she said. She described how the two main organizers were a husband-and-wife team. But one day the staffer was surprised when the couple asked for a meeting. Apparently, the husband had a problem with a federal agency and needed the senator's help. So, after the protesters left for the day, the couple went to the Senate office's conference room. After the meeting the wife proclaimed, "I can't believe it! You're so nice!"

6.5. How to Influence Legislators at Public Meetings

The best political education I received was not from a graduate school course or even from working the committee rooms of Capitol Hill during my time as a congressional aide. My best lessons came when I traveled off the Hill to attend my congressman's town hall meetings.

As a press secretary for a suburban Maryland congressman, I went to about 100 town hall meetings over a five-year period. It was at places like the VFW Hall in Glen Burnie where I saw firsthand how certain strategies led the congressman to say during the car ride home, "We have to look into that person's issue tomorrow."

Town hall meetings are excellent opportunities to get a legislator to make a public commitment or to agree to meet privately after the event. In addition to using the forums to espouse or defend their positions, many legislators use town hall meetings as a source for their own legislative agenda. "The best ideas I get for legislation come from town hall meetings," said one House Democratic subcommittee chairman. These meetings are usually announced to constituents through mailed postcards or emails.

Members of Congress are incredibly attentive to constituents who attend town hall meetings. One House Republican said he uses them like focus groups. "I'll offer up three to five issues," he said. "You get more off the cuff, unrehearsed reaction to issues. A town hall meeting is one way of getting off-the-street consensus."

Unfortunately, town hall meetings only tend to make the news when they become raucous affairs. In 2009, thousands of citizens attended town hall meetings to protest President Barack Obama's health care proposal. Similar protests erupted in the early days of President Donald Trump's two terms in office in 2017 and 2025. However, these headline-grabbing protests are rare. Most congressional town hall meetings are attended by 20–40 constituents and are marked by a polite dialogue between a legislator and her constituents.

Here are the top 10 strategies for taking advantage of these unique opportunities:

1. Be prepared. Most people don't approach their members of Congress with a well-researched, well-rehearsed pitch. Constituents who come to town hall meetings with thoughtful arguments, good data, and persuasive stories get remembered. And don't just read from some talking points provided by an interest group. Consider why you're making this case and prepare accordingly.

2. Tell a personal story. Members of Congress are always looking for firsthand accounts of the impact that policies have on their constituents. Think in advance of how a policy might affect you or your family, business, or community. (See Section 5.2 on the value of and how to build your personal story.)

3. Use numbers if you have them. As shown in Chart 3 (Section 5.4), someone representing other constituents—such as a union leader, company owner, or association president—is extremely influential to lawmakers. Use numbers by mentioning things like, "I have 50 employees," "I represent 100 people in my union," or "There are 500 people in my community affected by this bill." If multiple constituents are affected by a bill or issue, they'll take notice.

4. Be polite. Some constituents start a conversation with, "I pay your salary so you better listen to me." It doesn't matter if you're talking to your grocer or a public official—starting any conversation with another person in a rude manner is not a very tactful way to persuade them. As one House Democrat said, "I respect those who reason and are willing to have a dialogue instead of just shouting and pounding on the table."

5. Go in groups. Nothing says "listen to me" to a public official like a small mob. This is not to suggest that you should bring pitchforks and torches to your next town hall meeting, but a chorus is better than a solo performance.

6. Talk to staff. Every Member brings staff to town hall meetings. For members of the U.S. House, town hall meetings are often set up by the district director, the most important staff member in the district office. If you show up a little early to the meeting, you'll likely meet them. Tell them your story before the meeting (also ask a public question during the meeting) and get their business cards. You'll be developing a key relationship and creating a champion for your cause within the office.

7. Leave paper. Any documents passed to state-based staff will likely be forwarded to the legislative assistant in Washington who covers your issue. One U.S. senator takes the documents he collects at his town hall meetings and personally delivers them to his staff in his Washington office. When a staffer receives that document from her senator, where do you think those requests for help stack up on that assistant's to-do list?

8. Follow up politely. Politely persistent people persuade politicians. Congressional offices are often overworked, and failure to respond to a question posed at a town hall meeting may not be purposeful, but merely a byproduct of a busy staff member. Follow up a week or two after the meeting if you don't get a satisfactory or clear answer to your question.

9. Get your people to multiple meetings. When a legislator hears the same obscure question at two different meetings in two different locations they might exclaim, "Why is *everyone* asking about this?" In reality it was just two people, but to the legislator it signaled the tip of some impending iceberg—that there was a deeper problem afoot.

10. Provide feedback to professional lobbyists. After interacting with a lawmaker in the district, it is vital that constituents provide feedback on what happened to their Washington government relations office. Some groups provide feedback forms online; others just make their email addresses available to supporters. Even relaying your notes to a local contact, such as a state association, will ensure that an "accountability loop" is closed. The next time your professional lobbyist meets with a legislator he'll mention your town hall meeting question—and the public official will know that he can't say one thing back home and another thing in Washington.

6.6. Telephone Town Hall Meetings

Around 2010, telephone town hall meetings began to proliferate in the U.S. And it wasn't just elected officials and political candidates who utilized them. Sports teams, celebrities, and all sorts of public figures saw the value in conducting group conversations with constituents and fans. Especially during the COVID-19 pandemic, members of Congress made ample use of this technology to communicate valuable public service information to their constituents. In 2021 an estimated three million Americans participated in a telephone town hall with a member of Congress. Members of Congress especially like the raw interactions with constituents. "Telephone town halls give us a chance to ask questions on pressing issues and get a sense of the district's feeling," said a House chief of staff.

The technology and structure of these meetings are relatively simple. A tech vendor is hired to recruit and facilitate (technically) the meeting. Using a pre-determined list, the company will call thousands of people with a pre-recorded message. "Hi, I'm Representative John Smith, and I'm conducting a telephone town hall meeting right now. If you'd like to participate or listen in, just hit 1 or stay on the line." When you join the call, you might find that the meeting has already started, and the legislator is mid-sentence. The reason for this is that the lawmaker is likely reaching out to more than 10,000 constituents, and the technology doesn't exist to make 10,000 phone calls simultaneously—so the recruiting calls occur on a rolling basis.

If you do get a call like this, it will likely be in the evening around 7:00 p.m. Even though it will interrupt your routine, it's most advantageous to participate in the call. For members of the U.S. House, the average attendance for a telephone town hall meeting is between 3,000 and 8,000 people. When you join the call, you'll get instructions on how to ask a question—*and you should ALWAYS ask a question.* When you have an audience in the thousands, getting a politician to go on the record in front of a large crowd is the equivalent of chiseling their public position in cement. In a 60–90-minute forum, lawmakers can usually only field about ten questions from participants. If you are chosen to ask a question, you'll be placed in a virtual waiting room. A staff member will join you in the "private room," and ask three things: what's your name, where are you from, and what is the topic of your question. This is not an attempt to censor unpleasant topics or weed out opponents. In fact, lawmakers welcome mildly hostile questions in order to demonstrate their open-mindedness. "We purposely solicit opposing views because we want people to see him taking on those issues," said a House chief of staff. The purpose of this vetting is merely to determine whether the caller is a bona fide crackpot who might yell, swear, or otherwise disrupt the meeting.

Even if you request to ask a question and don't get called on, a congressional or state House staffer will likely follow up with you. This is yet another opportunity to build a relationship with that legislative office and get your issue on their radar.

Finally, you don't necessarily need to wait for your phone to ring to participate in a congressional telephone town hall meeting. Most members of Congress notify their e-newsletter subscribers in advance of upcoming telephone town halls. Signing up to receive a lawmaker's e-newsletter is not only the best way to get invited to one, but also a great way to keep up with what the lawmaker is doing.

The Potential of Telephone Town Hall Meetings to Improve Democracy

There is no single magic formula to improve our democracy and enhance trust in Congress. Yet, one promising tool is telephone town hall meetings. As noted, these are simply giant conference calls in which an elected official will talk with thousands of constituents. While it doesn't happen every time, research shows that if done well these interactive sessions can enhance constituents' understanding of government, faith in our democratic institutions, and even lead more people to vote.

In 2005 the Congressional Management Foundation partnered with academics at Harvard University, University of California-Riverside, and the Ohio State University to study the impact of telephone town halls.[17] Thirteen members of the House and Senate agreed to engage constituents in telephone town hall meetings using novel practices. First, the elected officials didn't run the show: the sessions were moderated by a neutral party. This led participants to feel like they were not part of a propaganda session. Second, constituents were provided a short nonpartisan summary of the issue that would be discussed—immigration (a gutsy choice, given how polarizing it can be). Finally, the selected audience was a representative sample of the state or district.

---

17 The research was published in various academic journals, and in an easy-to-read 2018 book, *Politics with The People: Building a Directly Representative Democracy*, by Michael A. Neblo, Kevin M. Esterling, and David M.J. Lazer.

The results were astounding.

- In before-and-after surveys, participants were asked if they trust the member of Congress to do the right thing, "all/most of the time," "some of the time," "never," and "don't know." The support for "all/most of the time" rose from 38 percent before the meeting to 52 percent afterwards.
- When asked if the lawmaker was "accessible" and "fair," participants were nearly twice as likely to use those words to describe the lawmaker as compared to a control group of constituents who did not attend the meeting.
- Job approval for the elected official rose from 46 percent before the meeting to 62 percent afterwards.
- When asked if the participants approved of how the lawmaker was handling the issue of immigration, approval nearly tripled from 20 percent approval to 58 percent.

For the constituents who are fortunate to have a state or federal legislator who makes themselves available in these free-for-all sessions, the experience can be richly rewarding and beneficial to American democracy.

6.7. Influencing Staff, and Why It's Important

If you visit Washington to meet with your congressional office, you might be to find yourself meeting not with the congresswoman herself or her chief of staff, but instead with an aide who doesn't look old enough to buy a drink, much less understand your issue. "People assume that if they jump right to the chief of staff, they'll get answers," said one Republican House chief of staff. "They are wasting their time."

The reality is that these young people are the best and brightest America has to offer. Capitol Hill is one of the most competitive work environments in America. Hundreds of resumes come in for every job posted. It's common for offices to receive more than 200 resumes for a legislative assistant opening. Those selected usually come from the best schools in the nation or the legislator's home state and have stellar academic records and multiple internships. When they arrive in Washington, they get handed a portfolio of complex issues they must master, work 12-hour days, and get paid about one-third less than they would earn in the private sector.

In the modern Congress (post–1960s), staff play an outsized role in policy decision-making, more than most Americans realize. Senator Edward Kennedy (D-Massachusetts), who served from 1962 to his death in 2009, witnessed this change. "Ninety-five percent of the nitty-gritty work of drafting [bills] and negotiating [their final form] is now done by staff," he wrote in his memoir. "That… marks an enormous shift of responsibility over the past forty or fifty years."[18]

Congressional staff are silent patriots who keep the system running. In Washington they are overwhelmingly young, single, and idealistic. The average work week is about 60 hours, and Saturday or evening duty is common (usually to catch up on answering constituent mail or to attend a local function in the state). If you spend some time around these people, you'll discover that there are some Americans who still respond to John F. Kennedy's appeal, "Ask not what your country can do for you, ask what you can do for your country."

When you meet with a staffer, build rapport in the same way you would with a legislator. Probe to determine how much the assistant genuinely knows about your issue and offer to educate them. Most of the time a smart legislative assistant will not commit to a position on the spot, unless the legislator has already decided the issue. But if you make a specific request, the staffer will invariably take it to the legislator for a response.

It's always a good idea to get a business card from the staffer. Follow up in a day or two with a thank-you email. Then, follow up again in two weeks to see if the legislator has decided on the issue. And, if you think that this cherubic public servant isn't worth your time, just remember: this little wunderkind is the legislator's chief advisor on the issue most important to you and may be the last person he speaks with before making a final decision on your request.

---

18 Edward M. Kennedy, *True Compass: A Memoir* (2009).

Finally, it's crucial for constituents to appreciate the role in-state staff play in lawmakers' decision-making. Sometimes, local staff have more influence than the DC-based legislative assistant. "Building relationships with state staff is important because disproportionally the things that move forward in Congress are things that are generated from the local community," said one Senate state director. "There is sometimes a difference of opinion in an office. People seem to think that congressional staff in an office think we all just agree, but there are internal debates. I see that difference starkly between state and DC staff. Sometimes we in the state can see stuff they just don't see in DC. On one major issue, because we're working with the local elected officials, business leaders, etc., we were able to shift the narrative internally, and we were able to change the senator's opinion," he said.

6.8. Advocacy During an Election Year

As this book has emphasized throughout, elected officials feel a moral and political obligation to listen to constituents. Yet, as Election Day approaches, the political imperative to be responsive grows even stronger for all the reasons you'd expect. This means that citizen-advocates can capitalize on legislators' interest in making voters happy close to Election Day.

Your level of involvement in a lawmaker's campaign will depend on how much you really like what the official stands for. It would be disingenuous to pretend to be a politician's friend when you despise their platform. But if you are in sync with their views, there are a couple of ways you can use election-year timing to your advantage.

Start by attending campaign events, like rallies or telephone town hall meetings run by the campaign staff. If you attend a larger event with hundreds of people, it's unlikely you'll get a one-on-one with the candidate. But just like in their official capacity, getting to know campaign staff is a good strategy for connecting with the lawmaker. If you raise a legislative issue or bill, they're likely to pass you off to the lawmaker's state or congressional legislative staff—which is good.

If you choose to increase your involvement, consider hosting a fundraiser at your home for the elected official. Be forewarned: campaign fundraisers require real effort. You'll be expected to invite potential donors from your network of friends and to foot the bill for catering. Yet doing so will ensure a stronger bond with that official.

One simple way to get the attention of a lawmaker, especially one about to start their first term in office, is to send them a written note of congratulations. You'd be surprised at how few constituents use this basic form of flattery, but it's almost certain to be seen by the lawmaker. (For more on this, see Section 5.10.)

Finally, never EVER mix campaign and official activities. If you contribute to a campaign, and then meet with the lawmaker or their official staff, it's illegal to connect the financial contribution to an official act. Doing so is always the quickest way to get booted out of the office, never again to see that official or their staff.

One constituent connected to a trade association was meeting with a senior Senate staffer to ask if the senator would cosponsor a bill. When the staffer said they were waiting to decide until after an upcoming hearing on the bill, the constituent said, "Well, given our $3,000 contribution in the last campaign we were expecting a different answer." The staffer replied, "Would you excuse me a minute?" A few minutes passed and in came the U.S. senator who bellowed, "I'm sending back your contribution, and you will never set foot in my office again!" That senator went on to serve another 22 years in the Senate.

6.9. Checklist for Preparing and Hosting an Event with an Elected Official

Politicians love attending well-planned and well-executed events. Yet the labor and choreography that goes into these affairs can be daunting. It's kind of like staging a theater production—except you don't get to do any rehearsals in advance of the show. Here is a checklist to consider when conducting an event with a legislator.[19]

Preparation and Planning

- Identify lawmaker(s) to attend. Be mindful not to invite too many politicians. Most elected officials prefer to be the biggest muckety-muck in the room.

- Identify resources (people, equipment) required to conduct the event.

- Create a project plan with assignments for all involved in planning and execution.

- Scout possible locations. Consider the visuals and the message they convey.

- List possible additional speakers.

- Consider inviting the media—but always check if that's okay with the staffs of the elected officials first.

- Draft a social media plan. Include posts before, during, and after the event.

- Draft a press advisory for pre-event distribution, including the who, what, where, when, and why of the event.

- Coordinate photography. You don't need a professional photographer, but photos for social media consumption are a must-have.

- Prepare contact lists of all participants with phone numbers and email addresses, and share them with all involved in planning the event.

- Determine who will greet elected officials when they arrive and how they will be briefed on any last-minute updates.

---

19 This list is adapted from the "Press Conference Checklist" in *Media Relations Handbook for Government, Associations, Nonprofits, and Elected Officials,* by Bradford Fitch and published by the Sunwater Institute.

Execution

- Distribute any talking points or press releases to the media.
- Post social media content.

Follow-Up

- Send thank-you notes to all participants and volunteers.
- Collect all social media and mainstream media coverage.
- Conduct an after-action review with your team, assessing what worked, what didn't, and what to do differently at a future event.

Chart 5 Survey of Congressional Staff

If you are not able to provide a firm answer to their request/ask, how FREQUENTLY is follow up conducted by the following?

If you are not able to provide a firm answer to their request/ask, how EFFECTIVE are these follow-up activities?

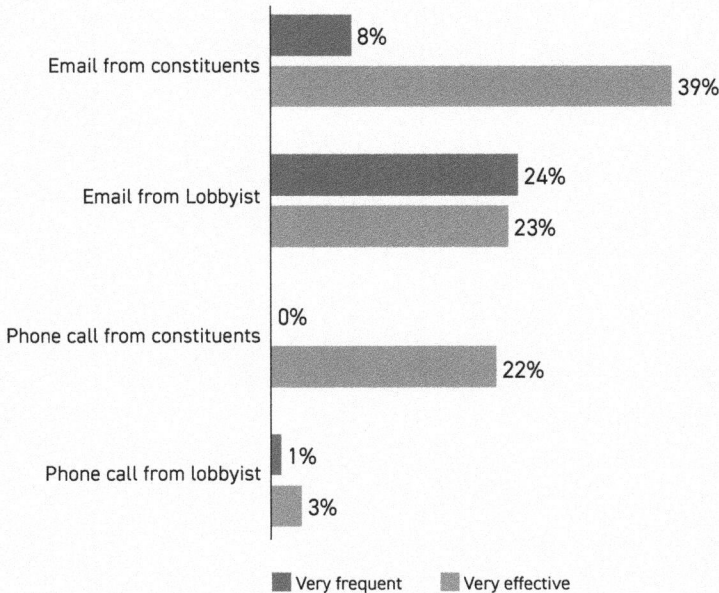

Email from constituents: 8%, 39%
Email from Lobbyist: 24%, 23%
Phone call from constituents: 0%, 22%
Phone call from lobbyist: 1%, 3%

Very frequent Very effective

Source: Congressional Management Foundation

121

Chapter 7
Communications

Use simple words everyone knows, then everyone will understand.

— Winston Churchill

The most common ways citizens interact with elected officials are through email, letters, social media, or phone calls. The cynical view is that as internet access and digital communications to Capitol Hill have grown, the value of these communications has diminished. Yet constituent communications are still an important method for connecting with lawmakers. "The most important thing that people should understand is that mail matters more than most constituents think it does," said one Republican senator. "There might be 100 different answers from 100 different senators, but each one will tell you the same basic thing: that mail has more of an impact than any citizen realizes," he said. Yet with about 50 million messages flooding Congress from constituents annually, the type and *quality* of communication matters greatly.

A good old-fashioned letter or email remains a valuable way to communicate with legislators. Incoming communications are reviewed and sorted daily by staff and interns into categories, date-stamped, and logged into an office database called a "Correspondence Management System." In October 2001, two members of Congress and several news organizations were sent letters containing the deadly toxin anthrax, killing five people. As a result, all postal communications sent to legislators' Washington offices are now scanned, digitized, and delivered electronically to each congressional office. For hand-written letters, images of the originals are sent to Congress.

Email is the most effective way to send a written communication to legislators.[20] As congressional offices enhance their technology, email is often quickly integrated into tracking systems, instantly notifying legislators of constituents' opinions. The most sophisticated software can even analyze how much of the email message was a template text drafted by a group organizing a campaign and how much was written by the sender. Thanks to the speed of delivery, ease of response, and flexibility to include links to other valuable persuasive components (such as video), email remains one of the most versatile and effective tools for advocates.

7.1. How to Write Letters and Emails to Legislators that Influence Decision-Making

What distinguishes good communications from weak ones isn't the method of delivery, but the writing. As noted in Chart 3 (Section 5.4), next to having a one-on-one meeting with your congresswoman, sending a personalized email or letter is one of the most effective ways to influence undecided lawmakers. "Constituent letters often raise issues that are not on our radar," said one House chief of staff. It is remarkable how easy it is to write an influential email to Congress, and how few people write good ones. Much of the communications that flow into congressional offices are either form emails drafted by lobbyists or angry rants. This is why when someone sends in a well-written argument, the note will often be put in a legislator's "to read" file. Below is a guide for constructing a model communication to a

---

20 The term "email" is used here, even though members of Congress shifted away from actual email addresses in the early 2000s. All "email" messages are now sent to Congress via webforms or similar technology—either through the website maintained by the member of Congress or a facilitating website from a trade association, nonprofit, or corporation, which then delivers the message to Congress.

legislator.

Paragraph 1 – Establish your standing. The emails and letters most likely to influence legislators are those from individuals who are personally affected by a policy, or have relevant knowledge of the impact. You see parents of children with diseases who start the letters with, "My child has juvenile diabetes, and I think we should increase research funding." It's a likely bet that the congressman is going to see that letter and respond quickly.

Paragraph 2 – Communicate a personal story. Why should this legislator listen to you (other than the fact the Constitution requires him to)? The *power* advocates possess rests in their personal story. Tell a story in a compelling way, communicating both emotion and fact. As noted in Section 5.2, personal stories usually beat out rational arguments with politicians.

Paragraph 3 – Include a specific "ask." As with every interaction with an elected official, be specific in what you request. "Please cosponsor this bill." "Please go on the House floor and speak on behalf of this project." A letter to a congressman from an earlier era had a specific ask while demonstrating the constituent's support. "Dear Congressman. I voted for you three times and I think you are wonderful. Please send me $900 at once so I can buy an icebox and repaint my car. Sincerely, John. PS. The three times I voted for you were in the election of 1946."[21] Perhaps not the best model for a public policy request, but certainly one the lawmaker would remember.

Paragraph 4 – Include local data. Lawmakers crave accurate, localized information on the impact of proposed policies or laws on their constituency. With hundreds of issues pending before Congress, legislators need reliable data on how their decisions might affect constituents. This doesn't mean you need to conduct a vast research project—do a quick survey of 10 or 20 people who share the same interests and provide those findings to the legislator.

Paragraph 5 – Communicate passion. Even if you don't have a vested interest in a policy question, you can still communicate how strongly you

----

21 Juliet Lowell, *Dear Mr. Congressman* (1948).

feel about it. Threats are not effective, but enthusiasm is. The occasional underlined sentence or exclamation point tells the legislator that crossing you may result in a newly minted volunteer for their opponent's campaign. Conversely, writing in ALL CAPS is the equivalent of shouting and is not effective.

One Republican congressman summed it up this way: "What I look for in communications is not just 'I'm for' or 'I'm against' something, I look for *why* you are for or against something."

7.2. Effective (and Ineffective) Phone Calls to Legislators

Many legislators review phone tallies when hot issues are before a legislature. Assistants are charged with recording the number of constituents who call "pro" and "con" on an issue, providing the lawmaker with an instant poll on a topic. It's far from scientific but still has value to a politician. Many members of Congress, after observing a harried staff assistant taking dozens of calls on an issue, will ask the young aide at the end of the day, "How mad are they?"

For the U.S. Congress, it's best to call the Washington office. Nearly all congressional offices base their constituent communications operation in Washington, so your call is most likely to be quickly logged with the right people. Keep the call short, one to three minutes. Long calls from constituents suggest a "wacky" factor and might result in your message being ignored.

Some groups also set up or hire phone banks to generate calls to lawmakers' offices. This can be effective *only if* the callers are trained on how to make the call. Congressional staff can spot canned, unmotivated callers in a split second. In contrast, when the callers who are identified have clear interests, are provided the right talking points, and are connected to offices over a short period of time (a couple of days), the impact can be powerful. A few do's and don'ts:

- *DO* note that you are a constituent early in the conversation. That triggers a response on the other end of the phone, "Oh, this call is important."

- *DO* reference a specific bill or decision that is pending with the legislator. Vague references will be ignored.

- *DO* give an email address (preferred) or street address and ask for a reply. This verifies that you are a constituent and ensures a degree of accountability.

- *DO* be polite. The Constitution gives you a right to raise the issue, but not to yell at some poor staff assistant.

- *DON'T* pretend to be some important muckety-muck if you're not. "I once went skeet shooting with the congressman's third cousin" isn't the ticket to greater influence.

- *DON'T* threaten with your vote, campaign contribution, or anything of value if the legislator doesn't do what you want. Any reference to the campaign given in an official setting will immediately disqualify the caller as a serious and ethical constituent.

7.3. How to Write Letters to the Editor that Get Published

Letters to the editor serve many purposes in public debate. They are used to respond to criticism, correct an inaccuracy, complain about the slant of coverage, point out a missing fact in a story, or amplify an element of the story in an interesting way. In the advocacy world, letters to the editor are excellent complements to directly contacting legislators and raising public awareness. They are also one of the best ways to get a legislator's attention.

As a congressional press secretary, I could hand my boss a stack of clips from the front page of every newspaper in the district that said he walked on water. And yet he'd often scan the reef of papers and find one line in a letter to the editor of a weekly paper with a circulation smaller than a church bulletin, and say to me: "Did you see what this guy said about me on page 37 in paragraph 4 opposite the ad for the furniture auction?" Legislators are creatures with egos, and they want to be loved by everyone. One or two lines of criticism (or praise) might seem meaningless in a broad effort to sway opinion, but if you mention the name of a member of Congress in a letter to the editor it will be read by the person you most want to influence: the legislator.

Here are the rules for writing letters to the editor that will get published.

First, editors are more likely to publish your letter if it's connected to a story that ran in the paper during the last week. In fact, it's almost impossible to get a letter to the editor published that does not reference a story or something timely and relevant in the community. If possible, cite the story you're responding to in the first sentence of your letter.

Second, keep the letters short—100 to 200 words, or two to four paragraphs. Every publication with a letter-to-the-editor section will have instructions on their website, including letter length. Succinct, strong, and powerful language is much more likely to gain an editor's attention than long-winded rants, or even thoughtful, but lengthy, arguments. Like a lawmaker, editors are much more attracted to stories from someone who has an *interest* or *connection* to an issue, rather than those just expressing an opinion. Those with a personal story to tell about an issue have an advantage over those who do not. Also, anyone who represents a group warrants attention. Even those who chair a small neighborhood committee are perceived to be speaking for others and are therefore good candidates for publication.

If you find compelling language on a website of an organization you support, use it as a foundation for your writing, but do not send it to the newspaper verbatim. Some grassroots organizations and political campaigns are smart about organizing letter-to-the-editor campaigns, and they are a valuable and ethical component of any lobbying effort. However, if an editor sees two letters with identical copy, he will consider the letter "manufactured" and will not run it. Use your own words to express your feelings.

Third, make sure to reference the legislator by name. If the lawmaker has ignored you or your issue, letters to the editor are a great way to get their attention. On the flip side, if the lawmaker has supported your issue, *definitely* write a letter to the editor. Publicly thanking an elected official in a local newspaper will get noticed by that official and probably everyone who works for her. It's also very wise to send a copy to the legislator's office (directed to their chief aide). Even if the letter isn't published, you will be sending a potent message that you have the power to influence thousands of voters. And the voice of one person in the letters-to-the-editor section has more credibility than a roomful of politicians.

Finally, if appropriate, let readers know how they can get involved. Some newspapers refuse to run website addresses. Include organization names or relevant clubs—anything that points a potential recruit in the right direction.

7.4 Using Social Media to Connect with Lawmakers

Nearly every elected official today is on social media. The most used platforms at the time of this writing are Facebook and X. Many also post on Instagram. Since the dawn of social media, politicians saw the new tools as a platform to communicate directly with constituents (avoiding those pesky media reporters).

Of course, in recent years, the dark side of social media has become all too clear, especially as it relates to politics. Lawmakers spend a lot of time debunking myths and correcting misinformation. It's reminiscent of the Mark Twain quote, "A lie can travel halfway around the world while the truth is putting on its shoes."

Members of Congress and their staff will use social media in ways they would never use traditional media. Every activity and utterance can be instantly broadcast to a wide and often receptive audience. Interestingly, a quick scan of most congressional social media accounts will show that members' posts in their districts are very different than those written in Washington. When they're in Washington and Congress is in session, the posts follow a predictable pattern: "We're great, they suck, here's why." The partisanship that we see daily is amplified on their social media accounts. But when lawmakers return home, their feed tells a different story. We get a wonderful overview of the diversity of their work. They're at a ribbon cutting of the new wing of the local hospital, talking to a group of high school civic students, or getting their picture taken with the prize-winning hog at the county fair.

For citizen-advocates, social media offers an amazing opportunity to hold lawmakers accountable, as it's one of the best ways to monitor their activities. You should sign up for the legislator's Facebook and X feeds. Additionally, Facebook has a "constituent badge" feature which shows lawmakers who represent you that you're a certified constituent. There are tradeoffs to using this feature. Once you sign up through the Facebook town hall tool, you'll see every person in government who represents you, and they'll know you're a constituent. The downside is that you must give Facebook your address, and they'll likely sell it to someone.

Elected officials are most interested in seeing the reaction of constituents to their posts, so if a lawmaker makes a comment or takes action on a cause you care about it's important for you to react and post immediately. And if you get a meaningful or interesting reply, you can share that with your network. "If they're reasonable, and a constituent, we respond on social media, and we like that engagement," said one House communications director. If you repost or write a fresh comment about a legislator's activity, always link to their Facebook page or include their X handle. That way your post will be seen by the person you most want to see it: the elected official.

How lawmakers view constituent posts varies widely by the interests and proclivities of that lawmaker. One House chief of staff said, "My boss is obsessed with his X account." I once conducted a "pop-up liquid focus group" with five Senate digital directors. (Buy a round of drinks for congressional staff and you can collect a lot of data.) The states their bosses represented varied in location and size. I asked how their bosses "consume" their social media feeds. One senator stayed on X all day, just seeing what people were saying about him. Another received weekly spreadsheets tabulating opinions. A third got quick anecdotal summaries from her staff while walking to votes.

Most politicians feed off this feedback because they crave public reaction and, ideally, public support for their views and work. Some years ago, I was waiting to appear on a C-SPAN program, and a member of Congress was on air in the studio answering questions from callers. Her press secretary was in the waiting room with me, watching both the broadcast and the reaction on (then) Twitter. "Oh, they liked that answer," she said. Moments later: "Oops, they don't like that answer." She was getting an instant *line-by-line* analysis of her boss's performance. As has been said many times in this book, elected officials crave constituent interaction, and social media offers immediate relief for that craving.

Finally, it should go without saying: please be polite. In open-ended survey responses from congressional staff, the most common word used to describe social media was "cesspool." Like any person, politicians will recoil and eventually ignore those who engage in withering rants.

Chart 6 Survey of Congressional Staff

If your Member of Congress has not arrived at a firm decision on an issue, how much influence might social media posts directed to your office (including posts on your office/Member platforms) from the following have on his/her decision?

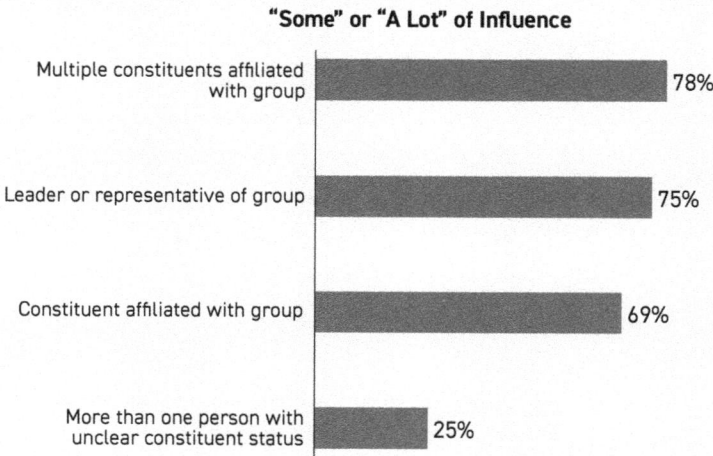

"Some" or "A Lot" of Influence

Multiple constituents affiliated with group — 78%

Leader or representative of group — 75%

Constituent affiliated with group — 69%

More than one person with unclear constituent status — 25%

Source: Congressional Management Foundation

7.5. Engaging Local Media to Support Your Advocacy Efforts

The only thing more intimidating than engaging with a politician is talking to a reporter. Former Vice President Hubert H. Humphrey said it best: "It's always a risk to speak to the press; they are likely to report what you say."

Yet, for most citizen-advocates and most causes, local media can be a valuable tool and ally. While the national media landscape has undergone significant transformation in the past few decades, what motivates and interests local media has not changed much. And while news consumption at the national level has shifted from national media outlets to social media feeds, trust in local media is still high. If a local kid wins the science fair and gets a trip to a national competition, it's still news. The great *New York Times* columnist, Russell Baker, wrote once that we shouldn't even call it "news." "Ninety-nine percent of what passes for *news* is actually nothing but *olds*," he said.

For a citizen-advocate, this means the same basic rules to gain media attention that worked 30 years ago still apply. And garnering local media coverage has many advantages. It promotes the value of your work to stakeholders. It could act as an inducement for more volunteers or funding. And, perhaps most importantly, it gets the attention of elected officials. Every politician will be grateful to the constituent who can get their picture in the news and associate them with a worthy cause.

Generally, local newspapers, radio stations, and TV stations need the following seven elements to consider covering a story.

1. Who are you? Journalists want to know your background and connection to the story to establish your credibility as a source. Any connection to a local group with a history of working in the community is a plus.

2. What is "new" about your story? Despite Russell Baker's quip, mainstream media is interested in reporting new things. A food bank hits a milestone in distributing meals; a hospital offers a new treatment to help kids; or the 4-H Club wins a state competition. There may also be a "news peg," some date or anniversary marking an event which the media deems newsworthy.

3. What is the narrative? Stories have characters, beginnings, middles, and endings. What is the arc of your story? Reporters love a good yarn, so spell it out for them in simple terms to get their attention.

4. What is the "picture"? Visuals triumph over all things in local media. Editors know that good pictures lead to clicks, subscriptions, and ratings. Paint the picture for the media outlet. Give them as

many details about the setting as possible. If you're pitching a TV station, make sure they understand the lighting in the location so they can have the correct equipment to record the interview or event.

5. Who will be in the story? Local media play favorites. They like to run stories with kids, animals, and old people. Boring men in business suits do not interest them (which is why politicians—mostly boring men in business suits—often stage events with seniors, children, and dogs). They like human interest stories that will grab readers' attention. The reason why every summer local papers run stories about parades and county fairs is because they usually involve all three. It may sound trite, but local media are rather uniform in their preferences.

6. When is this happening? Local media need daily if not hourly content. The best time to pitch a newspaper, radio station, or TV station is about a week before an event. If you try to gain their interest sooner, they'll forget; let it go until 24 hours before and they'll have already assigned their reporters to other stories.

7. Where is this happening? Local media is just that—local. They have a defined geographic area they cover, and they will not travel beyond that area.

Local media may involve you in ways you don't expect. A few years ago, a church was hosting an event with Rise Against Hunger, an international nonprofit that delivers millions of meals to impoverished nations using an innovative model. Rise Against Hunger provides the raw materials—rice, seasoning, dried vegetables, packaging, etc.—and a local partner recruits hundreds of volunteers to spend two to three hours packaging dry meals. An event organizer alerted the local paper that about 200 volunteers at the church would assemble 20,000 meals in two hours on a Sunday afternoon. "Would you like to send a reporter?" "No," the editor wrote back in an email. "But if you write up the story yourself and send some photos we'll likely run it!" The organizer found a former reporter in the church congregation and another volunteer whose hobby was photography. Sure enough, the newspaper ran the write-up and showcased a photo of a seven-year-old boy and his mom packaging meals bound for Haiti. You never know what kind of media attention you can get to highlight your cause if you don't ask.

7.6. Why Petitions Usually Fail to Influence Congress

There are groups that lobby Congress who love petitions. Many websites have popped up offering visitors the chance to create their own petition and send it to Congress. Regrettably, many of these sites are simply "data mining" operations. They convince you to give them your email address and identify some issue that interests you and then sell the data to a group that will seek your donation or support. Few congressional offices read or acknowledge petitions unless they are hand-signed, with constituent addresses included, and demonstrate a strong opinion (with big numbers) on an issue relevant to the office. The best way, and virtually only way, to use petitions in an advocacy campaign is as a prop. Get a few thousand folks to pen their name and address on a statement, then ship the rumpled, stained, and loosely wrapped package to your professional-advocate in Washington. She'll use it the next time she has a meeting with a legislator to demonstrate grassroots support or opposition for an issue back home.

How One Letter Reached the Oval Office and Fed a Million People

In 2004, President George W. Bush was signing a bill related to world hunger in the White House Rose Garden. Among those in attendance was Senator Richard Lugar (R-Indiana), chairman of the Senate Foreign Relations Committee, and Dr. David Beckmann, president of Bread for the World, a church-based nonprofit that seeks to reduce hunger and fight AIDS worldwide.

Dr. Beckmann saw an opportunity to give a pitch to the leader of the free world for another program close to his organization's heart, the Millennium Challenge Account, which, if supported by the president and fully funded by the Congress, would help relieve hunger in the eight poorest nations in the world. It had received $1 billion in funding in 2004, but like any good advocate, David Beckmann wanted more.

He approached the president in the White House Rose Garden and asked him to increase funding for the Millennium Challenge Account, pointing out how much good just a little additional funding could do. President Bush asked his friend Senator Lugar, chairman of the Senate Foreign Relations Committee, what he thought of this program. Senator Lugar replied, "You know, I am just now responding to a letter from a constituent, Mrs. Connie Wick of Indianapolis. She is saying just what you are saying, David, that we should fully fund the Millennium Account, the AIDS initiative, and not cut funding for ongoing programs to help poor people."

At the time, Connie Wick was 83 years old and lived in the Robin Run Retirement Community on Happy Hollow Road in Indianapolis, Indiana. She was not a wealthy contributor to a political party, she had never run for public office, and did not have legions of followers. She was one voice, one person, who felt that America should do more to help feed the hungry. In the president's proposed budget for the following year, the Millennium Account funding rose from $1 billion a year to $2.5 billion.

Perhaps it's just a coincidence. Or perhaps the president of the United States, when he was considering the budget for the next year, had Connie Wick's words in mind. As you consider your role in the democratic process, remember that you have the power to change the world. And remember the most important lesson our Founders taught us: Politics is too important to be left to politicians.

7.7. Thank or Spank? After-the-Vote Communications

After the issue has been decided and the votes cast, is there value in communicating with legislators to either praise them (thank) or condemn them (spank)? The answer is a resounding "YES!"

Thank-you notes to legislators are a rarity in public office. Any time one is sent to a member of Congress it is immediately put at the top of his "to read" pile. It might even be read aloud at the next staff meeting. Then, the next time you or your group has an issue before that legislator, he and his staff are going to start the discussion with that fond memory in mind.

Conversely, it is important for you to communicate your disappointment with legislators who do not support you. This should be done politely and professionally, but firmly. Avoid threats such as, "I'm not going to vote for you now." It comes across to the legislator and staff as petulant. Instead, express the wish that the *next time* the issue comes up, you hope he will reconsider his position. Or perhaps another issue could arise in the future on which you could agree. The goal here is to make sure the legislator knows that he is accountable—and that you're watching. This has a profound psychological effect on public officials and forces them to be ever mindful of those individuals and groups who persistently and politely never let them out of their sight.

7.8. The Magic of Combining Tactics

At the beginning of the 20th century, neurophysiologist Dr. Charles Sherrington was curious about dogs. He wanted to know why, when you rubbed a dog's belly, it would invariably shake its back leg. Dr. Sherrington discovered that you could produce the same result if you slightly rubbed the dog's belly while simultaneously patting his head.[22]

Well, politicians are a little like dogs. They respond to intense pressure of one kind, or they respond to moderate pressure from a multitude of sources. When legislators are confronted with a difficult decision, they bring together senior staff to get input. The legislative director might say, "We've gotten 50 emails in favor of this bill." The district director might say, "You got two questions about the bill at your recent telephone town hall meetings." The press secretary could say, "There have been three letters to the editor endorsing it." At that point, there's no further debate—the legislator would say, "OK, let's do it… What's next?"

---

22 This connection between advocacy and Dr. Sherrington's work was first discovered by Dr. Alan Rosenblatt, adjunct professor at George Washington University's Graduate School of Political Management, and one of the early experts in digital advocacy.

Epilogue

As a Capitol Hill staffer, I gave tours of the U.S. Capitol building to constituent visitors who came to see Washington. I was often struck by how we inhabitants of the institution took this magnificent building for granted. Staff treated the U.S. Capitol as an office building, members of Congress treated it like an exclusive club, but our constituents treated it like a shrine, and their trip to Washington like a pilgrimage to the birthplace of democracy.

Most parents brought their children to Washington to imbue them with some sense of citizenship—the idea that as you grow up you have a responsibility to the greater good and not just to yourself. One of my great challenges and joys of these tours was trying to explain government to very small children, and I found the secret formula by breaking government down to its most basic function.

"You know that Mommy and Daddy make rules for you," I would say to a 5-year-old, and she would nod with a depressed look. "Well, this is the place and the people who make the rules for Mommy and Daddy." Suddenly, my young advocate would have this "ah-ha" moment. It hadn't occurred to her that the people who were at the center of her universe also had to answer to some higher authority. Suddenly a host of imperial dictates dealing with bedtime rituals, candy distribution, bathing schedules—all were up for grabs and had the potential for review, if only one knew how to lobby just right. "I need to see these people," they would show in their eyes, "We got some things to talk about."

At the risk of sounding paternalistic, many citizens have not yet had the "ah-ha" moment my young tourists experienced. They've yet to realize that all the rules that govern their lives—from the cleanliness of their water to how their children are educated to how much they are taxed—are all up for grabs. It merely requires the will to get involved, and a little know-how on what to do. This book has offered some of the latter, while hopefully inspiring you to believe that your involvement will have meaning.

Great leaders have always understood that the ultimate power in a democracy rests with the people, not with congressman or presidents or the special interest lobbyists. "Public sentiment is everything," President Abraham Lincoln said. "With public sentiment, nothing can fail, without it, nothing can succeed." The next time you want to rant at something the government has done, remember Lincoln's words and don't just rant. Pick up a pen, call a friend, or send an email. Give purpose to your passion, knowing that you and others like you have the power to change the world. Remember Margaret Mead: "Never doubt that a small group of committed citizens can change the world... indeed, it is the only thing that ever has."

Appendix A
Glossary of Congressional Terms[23]

Term	Explanation
Amendment	A proposal by a member of Congress to alter the text of a measure or bill.
Appropriations	Provision of law providing budget authority that permits federal agencies to incur obligations and make payments out of the Treasury. This term is sometimes called the "budget" by the media, however, a "budget resolution" is a different legislative vehicle.
Authorization	Provision of law that establishes or continues authority for how a program or agency functions. In essence, it is a law that tells the federal agency what to do.
Bill	Measure that becomes law when passed in identical form by both chambers of Congress and signed into law by the president or alternatively passed over the president's veto by overriding it.

23 Some of the terms and descriptions are from *Congressional Deskbook: The Practical and Comprehensive Guide to Congress*, by Michael L. Koempel and Judy Schneider, and published by the Sunwater Institute.

Budget Resolution	Legislation, agreed to by both the House and Senate, which is a broad outline of spending for the entire federal government. The budget resolution does not authorize or appropriate funds. Rather, it sets the procedural limits for the funding bill as well as the parameters for a final reconciliation bill which "reconciles" the program outline in the budget resolution to enact final law. A budget resolution is only passed by the Congress and is not signed by the president. For a reconciliation bill to be considered an identical budget resolution must be passed by both the House and Senate.
Chairman's Mark	Recommendation by the committee or subcommittee chair of the measure to be considered by the committee or subcommittee, usually drafted as a bill.
Cloture	Process used in the Senate to end a filibuster. Cloture requires 60 affirmative votes for legislation and 51 votes for presidential nominees.
Committee Report	Document accompanying a measure or bill when reported by a committee to the full House or Senate. It contains an explanation of the provisions of the measure, arguments for its approval, and other information. While a committee report does not have the same enforceable powers of a law, report language can guide federal agencies (e.g., conduct a research study), and can be used by the courts to interpret the legislative intent of Congress. Reports may not be amended in the full House or Senate.
Conference Committee	Temporary joint committee created to resolve differences between the chambers on a measure or bill.
Congressional Budget Office (CBO)	The Congressional Budget Office (CBO) provides the Congress with objective, nonpartisan analyses and estimates related to federal economic and budgetary decisions. For every major bill reported to the House or Senate, the CBO issues a report showing how that legislation would affect spending by or revenue to the federal government as compared to current law, typically over a ten-year period. This estimate is called a "CBO score."

Congressional Research Service (CRS)	Congressional agency based in the Library of Congress that serves Congress throughout the legislative process by providing comprehensive and reliable legislative research and analysis that is objective, authoritative, and confidential. CRS independently produces reports to Congress on relevant topics, and CRS staff can provide custom research or respond to individual requests by congressional offices.
Continuing Resolution (CR)	Type of appropriations bill which maintains funding for the government, normally for a defined, shorter period of time.
Dear Colleague	Communications vehicles written by members of Congress (drafted by their aides), usually in the form of a one- to two-page letter distributed to every member office in that chamber. They are often written in plain language, asking colleagues to support a cause, issue, or pending legislation.
Democratic Caucus	Term used by House and Senate Democrats to describe their organizing body in their respective chambers.
Discharge Petition	Procedure to remove a measure from a House committee to which it was referred and make it available for a floor vote. To succeed, the petition must be signed by a majority of House members. Because it bypasses the regular legislative process and challenges House leadership it is rarely successful. The Senate has no similar procedure.
Discretionary Spending	Spending provided in, and controlled by, annual appropriations acts. This is the portion of the federal budget Congress debates each year and passes into law through appropriations bills (e.g., Defense Department, food stamps, healthcare research). It represents about 26 percent of the annual federal government spending.
Earmark	Spending proposed or approved within an appropriations bill for a specific purpose and usually directed to a recipient (e.g., a city government, hospital, or school system). Known as "Community Project Funding" in the House and "Congressionally-Directed Spending" in the Senate, these projects are requested by individual members of Congress.
Filibuster	Tactic in the Senate to delay or defeat a measure by engaging in unlimited debate and other means. Sixty votes are required to end a filibuster for legislation and 51 votes for nominees, known as Cloture.

Government Accountability Office (GAO)	Congressional agency which gathers information to help Congress determine how effectively executive branch agencies are doing their jobs. Report topics are determined by GAO leadership, requests from members of Congress, or mandated by law.
Hearing	Session or meeting conducted by congressional committee to exercise their oversight or legislative functions.
Lame-Duck Session	Session of Congress held after the election but prior to the swearing in of the next Congress. *The Congressional Globe* used "lame duck" to describe "broken down politicians" back in 1863, and it started to appear in newspaper articles referencing politics not long after.
Markup	Meeting by a committee or subcommittee during which members offer, debate, and vote on amendments to a measure or bill with the purpose of advancing the legislation to the House or Senate floor.
Nondiscretionary (or Mandatory) Spending	Spending mandated by law to be spent on services/payments to recipients regardless of the amount. Eligibility is determined by law and administered by rules established by federal and state governments. Spending includes Social Security, Medicare, and Medicaid, and represents about two-thirds of the annual federal government spending (as of 2025). Changes to eligibility and amounts can only be made through acts of Congress signed into law, often through a reconciliation bill. Mandatory spending is not considered by Congress on an annual basis.
Omnibus Bill	A measure or bill that combines the provisions related to several disparate subjects into a single bill. Examples include omnibus appropriations, bills which contain two or more of the 12 annual appropriations bills.
One-Minute Speech	Short speeches that may be conducted outside of the regular legislative order by members of the U.S. House, usually before the legislative business of the day.
Recess (District Work Period)	A period when a chamber is not in session for legislative business and no floor votes are held. Members of the House and Senate are usually working in their districts and states during this time.

Reconciliation Bill	A reconciliation bill is used to implement the policies set forth in a congressional budget resolution. While the budget resolution offers broad financial targets for federal programs and tax policy, the reconciliation bill includes specific changes to those taxes and programs. It is often the only way to amend entitlement programs and change tax law. In the Senate, reconciliation bills follow strict rules dictating that all provisions must affect federal spending, and provisions that do not do so (e.g. raising the minimum wage) are ruled out of order and stricken from the bill. By limiting debate time in the Senate, the procedure allows for finalization of a bill with only 51 votes (or 50 votes with the vice president providing the tie-breaking vote). Like all bills, a reconciliation bill must be signed by the president to become law. In recent years, this process has only been used when the same party holds the presidency and a majority in both chambers of Congress.
Republican Conference	Term used by House and Senate Republicans to describe their organizing body in their respective chambers.
Rider	Term used for an amendment which is attached to or amends a measure or bill.
Rule (Closed)	Procedure for consideration of a bill in the U.S. House with no amendments allowed.
Rule (Modified)	Procedure for consideration of a bill in the U.S. House with a specified set of amendments for consideration and votes as determined by the House Rules Committee.
Rule (Open)	Procedure for consideration of a bill in the U.S. House where all members are allowed to offer amendments as long as they comply with the rules of the House. This can lead to an unlimited set of amendments for consideration and votes and is rarely used.
Rules Committee (House)	Committee in the U.S. House which determines how a bill will be considered on the House floor. The Rules Committee determines the number of amendments, which amendments will be considered, and the length of time for debate. Its membership is determined by the Speaker of the House.
Special Order	Type of speech conducted in the U.S. House after legislative business has concluded for the day. Both parties are allowed up to 60 minutes to give speeches, often with multiple members speaking on a pre-determined topic.

Suspension of the Rules	Procedure by which bills may avoid committee consideration and be taken directly to the U.S. House floor. Debate time is limited to a total of 40 minutes and passage requires a two-thirds vote by the House. Due to this high threshold bills considered this way tend to either be noncontroversial or have broad bipartisan support.
Veto	Power vested in the president to reject bills passed by the Congress. Two-thirds votes by both chambers are required to override a presidential veto. If a veto is overridden, the legislation becomes law.

Appendix B
Good Books on the U.S. Congress

Thousands of books have been written about the U.S. Congress, both for the general reader and the political science community. For readers of this book, I've included below a smattering of texts that I found particularly good at explaining how America's democratic institution functions. They are in chronological order of publication date.

Home Style: House Members in Their Districts, by Richard Fenno (1978). Written by the renowned University of Rochester political scientist, this book remains the granddaddy of all books on Congress. During an eight-year period Fenno traveled with 18 members of Congress in their districts. And while uninformed pundits may say Congress has changed drastically over the last five decades, what motivates and drives the vast majority of legislators has not.

All Politics Is Local, by Tip O'Neill and Gary Hymel (1993). This book may be guilty of explaining an earlier era of Congress, but that doesn't diminish its value and fun. O'Neill was in Congress for 34 years and Speaker of the House for ten years. Written with homespun humor, O'Neill offers lessons that range from Machiavelli to his own history as a Boston political brawler and provides an insider's view of congressional leadership.

Reclaiming Our Democracy: Every Citizen's Guide to Transformational Advocacy, by Sam Daley-Harris (1993). If the reader did not get enough lessons in democracy from this book, Daley-Harris's terrific book is your next stop. Updated in 2024, the book goes beyond basic citizen-advocate training and offers guidance and wonderful case studies on grassroots organizing.

Act of Congress: How America's Essential Institution Works, and How It Doesn't, by Robert Kaiser (2014). This book has a remarkable origin story. Veteran *Washington Post* reporter Robert Kaiser approached Rep. Barney Frank, the powerful chair of the House Finance Committee, with an astonishing request: full access to the inner workings of the committee as it drafted a sweeping overhaul of America's financial services laws in response to the banking crisis of 2008. That meant all major internal documents developed during the committee process, on-the-record interviews with him and his key staff, and debriefs after every key meeting... and Barney Frank said "Sure!" The resulting volume is one of the *only* insider's views of how a major piece of legislation is enacted in the modern congressional era. Readers will get a front-row seat to the legislative process, meeting the heroes, villains, geniuses, and idiots that inhabit our national legislature.

Al Franken, Giant of the Senate, by Al Franken (2017). If the reader can put aside Senator Franken's (D-Minnesota) rather ignoble departure from the U.S. Senate, you'll get an informed and hilarious view of what it's like to work as a senator through this text. This book perfectly nails the daily interplay and relationships between members of Congress and their staffs (which range from brilliant assistance to enabling to obsequiousness to derision). Along the way you'll inevitably be drawn to Franken, both as a public servant and an accomplished storyteller.

Congress at a Crossroads: Retiring Members of Congress Tell Us What's Right, What's Wrong—And How to Fix It, by Mark Sobol and Leonard Steinhorn (2020). There are hundreds of books on what's wrong with Congress and only a few on how to fix the institution. Through FMC, the Former Members of Congress Association, the researchers interviewed 31 recently retired members of Congress in 2018 and 2019, exploring serious contributors to congressional gridlock: polarization, institutional dysfunction, media echo chambers, and the erosion of relationships between colleagues. For the serious student of practical solutions to complex problems, this 44-page report offers a glimpse into how to fix Congress.

Recommendations from the Select Committee on the Modernization of Congress (2022). As noted earlier in this book, the Select Committee on the Modernization of Congress was the most successful effort to improve the U.S. Congress since the 1970s. Its final report includes 202 recommendations, which the House is pursuing through a new, bipartisan Subcommittee on Modernization and Innovation. It's wonky reading that drills into the mundane details of lawmaking and legislative process. Yet, to improve our legislature, America needs public servants like those on the Select Committee and Subcommittee willing to engage in the unglamorous but essential task of reform.

Why Congress (Studies in Postwar American Political Development), by Philip A. Wallach (2023). Written by a former congressional staffer and think tank fellow, Wallach's book is at its best showing case studies from the past 50 years of Congress actually getting stuff done. He shares the ingredients for a functional national legislature, and offers some vision on what could improve the House and Senate.

Congress Overwhelmed: The Decline in Congressional Capacity and Prospects for Reform, edited by Timothy M. LaPira, Lee Drutman, and Kevin R. Kosar (2024). If you want to know what's really wrong with Congress, this book is for you. If I have one knock on it, it's this: the essays are VERY depressing. Various researchers and political scientists focus on the Congress's capacity (or lack thereof) to solve problems and go into detail on how Congress as an institution has declined in the last few decades. They aptly diagnose problems with congressional capacity, unequal power differential with the executive branch, and the role of congressional staff.

Appendix C
The Advocate's Pledge

When training groups who are about to descend on Capitol Hill for meetings with their lawmakers, I always ask them to take what I call The Advocate's Pledge. I wrote the pledge because simply *knowing* the right strategies does not ensure that volunteers will implement them. Stating the following boldface sentences—out loud and in front of their colleagues—will increase the likelihood that they'll *commit* and follow through.

Article 1: I will politely petition my legislator with all appropriate measures. This reminds advocates to be well mannered and rational in their dealings with legislators and to use every available means to influence policy (including in-person meetings, email, and attendance at town hall meetings).

Article 2: Under the Constitution, my legislator must listen to me... but I must know what I'm talking about. Yes, according to the First Amendment, advocates have a right to petition the government for a "redress of grievances." But if advocates want government to respond in the desired manner, they must know the issues and clearly communicate the impact of what they desire on a community or industry.

Article 3: I will encourage my fellow citizens to aid in our cause. Social media makes creating networks easier than ever. Nearly every grassroots software tool used by trade associations and nonprofit groups has a tell-a-friend feature that allows users to build connections instantly.

Article 4: Success is realized in both the result and my participation in the democratic process. Of course, winning is better than losing. But just because advocates suffer defeat with one legislative battle doesn't mean they're out of the game forever. It takes an average of seven years to pass a bill into law. Patience is more than a virtue. It's a job requirement.

What's more, by participating in the democratic process, your advocates send an important message to their member of Congress: "I'm watching." Accountability is the foundation of democracy. Just by being involved, you make a difference.

Appendix D
Legislative Process Flowchart

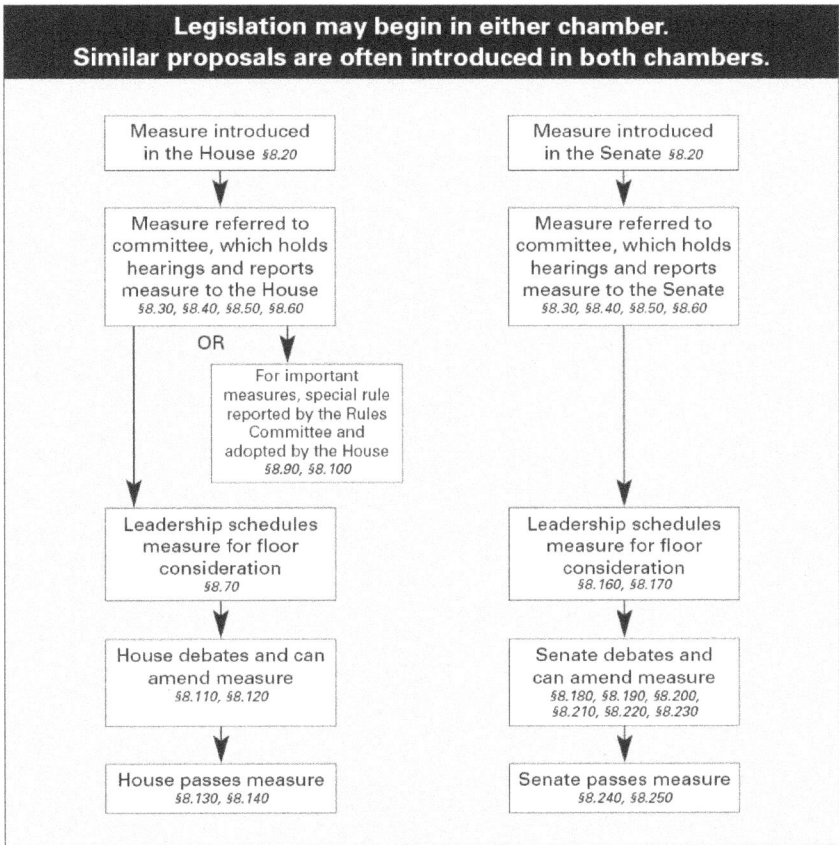

Legislation may begin in either chamber. Similar proposals are often introduced in both chambers.

Measure introduced in the House *§8.20*	Measure introduced in the Senate *§8.20*
Measure referred to committee, which holds hearings and reports measure to the House *§8.30, §8.40, §8.50, §8.60*	Measure referred to committee, which holds hearings and reports measure to the Senate *§8.30, §8.40, §8.50, §8.60*
OR — For important measures, special rule reported by the Rules Committee and adopted by the House *§8.90, §8.100*	
Leadership schedules measure for floor consideration *§8.70*	Leadership schedules measure for floor consideration *§8.160, §8.170*
House debates and can amend measure *§8.110, §8.120*	Senate debates and can amend measure *§8.180, §8.190, §8.200, §8.210, §8.220, §8.230*
House passes measure *§8.130, §8.140*	Senate passes measure *§8.240, §8.250*

Measures must pass both the House and the Senate in identical form before being presented to the President.		
One chamber agrees to the other chamber's version *§8.260*	Each chamber appoints Members to a conference committee, which reconciles differences and agrees to a conference report *§8.280*	House and Senate exchange amendments to bill and reach agreement *§8.270*
House approves conference report		Senate approves conference report

Legislation presented to the President.			
President signs measure	If President does not sign measure into law within 10 days *§8.290*		President vetoes measure
Measure becomes law	If Congress is in session, measure becomes law	If Congress is not in session, measure does not become law ("pocket veto")	Measure does not become law, unless both chambers override veto by 2/3 majority

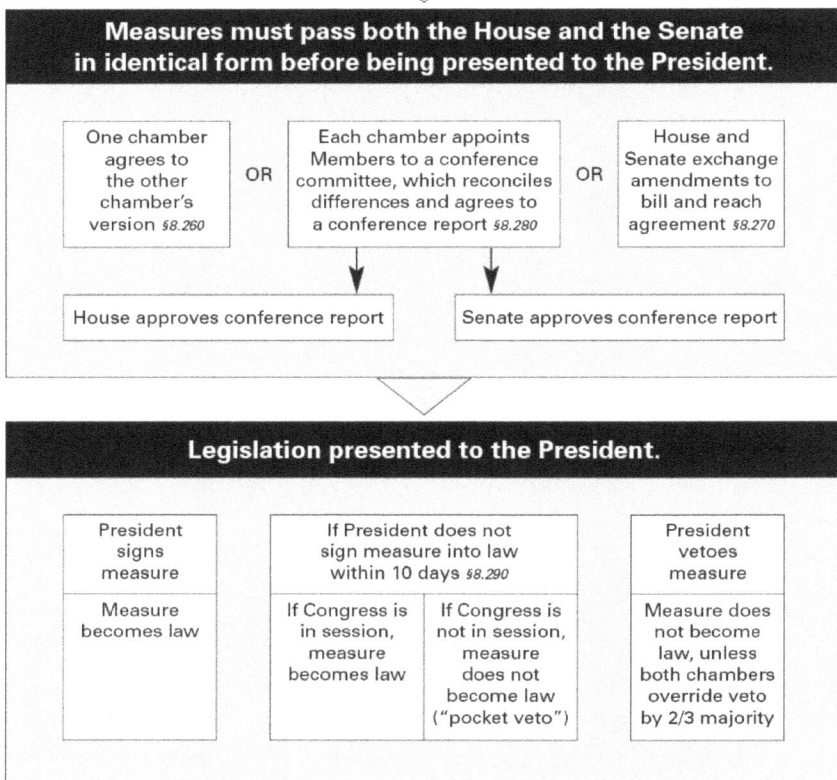

Sources: U.S. Senate; U.S. House of Representatives; and the *Congressional Deskbook*, by Michael Koempel and Judy Schneider (6th ed., 2012).

Appendix E
The U.S. Constitution and Amendments

We the People of the United States, in Order to form a more perfect Union, establish Justice, insure domestic Tranquility, provide for the common defence, promote the general Welfare, and secure the Blessings of Liberty to ourselves and our Posterity, do ordain and establish this Constitution for the United States of America

Article. I.

SECTION. 1

All legislative Powers herein granted shall be vested in a Congress of the United States, which shall consist of a Senate and House of Representatives.

SECTION. 2

The House of Representatives shall be composed of Members chosen every second Year by the People of the several States, and the Electors in each State shall have the Qualifications requisite for Electors of the most numerous Branch of the State Legislature.

No Person shall be a Representative who shall not have attained to the Age of twenty five Years, and been seven Years a Citizen of the United States, and who shall not, when elected, be an Inhabitant of that State in which he shall be chosen.

[Representatives and direct Taxes shall be apportioned among the several States which may be included within this Union, according to their respective Numbers, which shall be determined by adding to the whole Number of free Persons, including those bound to Service for a Term of Years, and excluding Indians not taxed, three fifths of all other Persons.]* The actual Enumeration shall be made within three Years after the first Meeting of the Congress of the United States, and within every subsequent Term of ten Years, in such Manner as they shall by Law direct. The Number of Representatives shall not exceed one for every thirty Thousand, but each State shall have at Least one Representative; and until such enumeration shall be made, the State of New Hampshire shall be entitled to chuse three, Massachusetts eight, Rhode-Island and Providence Plantations one, Connecticut five, New-York six, New Jersey four, Pennsylvania eight, Delaware one, Maryland six, Virginia ten, North Carolina five, South Carolina five, and Georgia three.

When vacancies happen in the Representation from any State, the Executive Authority thereof shall issue Writs of Election to fill such Vacancies.

The House of Representatives shall chuse their Speaker and other Officers; and shall have the sole Power of Impeachment.

SECTION. 3

The Senate of the United States shall be composed of two Senators from each State, [chosen by the Legislature thereof,]* for six Years; and each Senator shall have one Vote.

Immediately after they shall be assembled in Consequence of the first Election, they shall be divided as equally as may be into three Classes. The Seats of the Senators of the first Class shall be vacated at the Expiration of the second Year, of the second Class at the Expiration of the fourth Year, and of the third Class at the Expiration of the sixth Year, so that one third may be chosen every second Year; [and if Vacancies happen by Resignation, or otherwise, during the Recess of the Legislature of any State, the Executive thereof may make temporary Appointments until the next Meeting of the Legislature, which shall then fill such Vacancies.]*

No Person shall be a Senator who shall not have attained to the Age of thirty Years, and been nine Years a Citizen of the United States, and who shall not, when elected, be an Inhabitant of that State for which he shall be chosen

The Vice President of the United States shall be President of the Senate, but shall have no Vote, unless they be equally divided.

The Senate shall chuse their other Officers, and also a President pro tempore, in the Absence of the Vice President, or when he shall exercise the Office of President of the United States

The Senate shall have the sole Power to try all Impeachments. When sitting for that Purpose, they shall be on Oath or Affirmation. When the President of the United States is tried, the Chief Justice shall preside: And no Person shall be convicted without the Concurrence of two thirds of the Members present.

Judgment in Cases of Impeachment shall not extend further than to removal from Office, and disqualification to hold and enjoy any Office of honor, Trust or Profit under the United States: but the Party convicted shall nevertheless be liable and subject to Indictment, Trial, Judgment and Punishment, according to Law.

SECTION. 4

The Times, Places and Manner of holding Elections for Senators and Representatives, shall be prescribed in each State by the Legislature thereof; but the Congress may at any time by Law make or alter such Regulations, except as to the Places of chusing Senators.

The Congress shall assemble at least once in every Year, and such Meeting shall be [on the first Monday in December,]* unless they shall by Law appoint a different Day.

SECTION. 5.

Each House shall be the Judge of the Elections, Returns and Qualifications of its own Members, and a Majority of each shall constitute a Quorum to do Business; but a smaller Number may adjourn from day to day, and may be authorized to compel the Attendance of absent Members, in such Manner, and under such Penalties as each House may provide.

Each House may determine the Rules of its Proceedings, punish its Members for disorderly Behaviour, and, with the Concurrence of two thirds, expel a Member.

Each House shall keep a Journal of its Proceedings, and from time to time publish the same, excepting such Parts as may in their Judgment require Secrecy; and the Yeas and Nays of the Members of either House on any question shall, at the Desire of one fifth of those Present, be entered on the Journal.

Neither House, during the Session of Congress, shall, without the Consent of the other, adjourn for more than three days, nor to any other Place than that in which the two Houses shall be sitting.

SECTION. 6

The Senators and Representatives shall receive a Compensation for their Services, to be ascertained by Law, and paid out of the Treasury of the United States. They shall in all Cases, except Treason, Felony and Breach of the Peace, be privileged from Arrest during their Attendance at the Session of their respective Houses, and in going to and returning from the same; and for any Speech or Debate in either House, they shall not be questioned in any other Place.

No Senator or Representative shall, during the Time for which he was elected, be appointed to any civil Office under the Authority of the United States, which shall have been created, or the Emoluments whereof shall have been encreased during such time; and no Person holding any Office under the United States, shall be a Member of either House during his Continuance in Office.

SECTION. 7

All Bills for raising Revenue shall originate in the House of Representatives; but the Senate may propose or concur with Amendments as on other Bills

Every Bill which shall have passed the House of Representatives and the Senate, shall, before it become a Law, be presented to the President of the United States; If he approve he shall sign it, but if not he shall return it, with his Objections to that House in which it shall have originated, who shall enter the Objections at large on their Journal, and proceed to reconsider it. If after such Reconsideration two thirds of that House shall agree to pass the Bill, it shall be sent, together with the Objections, to the other House, by which it shall likewise be reconsidered, and if approved by two thirds of that House, it shall become a Law. But in all such Cases the Votes of both Houses shall be determined by Yeas and Nays, and the Names of the Persons voting for and against the Bill shall be entered on the Journal of each House respectively, If any Bill shall not be returned by the President within ten Days (Sundays excepted) after it shall have been presented to him, the Same shall be a Law, in like Manner as if he had signed it, unless the Congress by their Adjournment prevent its Return, in which Case it shall not be a Law

Every Order, Resolution, or Vote to which the Concurrence of the Senate and House of Representatives may be necessary (except on a question of Adjournment) shall be presented to the President of the United States; and before the Same shall take Effect, shall be approved by him, or being disapproved by him, shall be repassed by two thirds of the Senate and House of Representatives, according to the Rules and Limitations prescribed in the Case of a Bill.

SECTION. 8

The Congress shall have Power To lay and collect Taxes, Duties, Imposts and Excises, to pay the Debts and provide for the common Defence and general Welfare of the United States; but all Duties, Imposts and Excises shall be uniform throughout the United States;

To borrow Money on the credit of the United States;

To regulate Commerce with foreign Nations, and among the several States, and with the Indian Tribes;

To establish an uniform Rule of Naturalization, and uniform Laws on the subject of Bankruptcies throughout the United States;

To coin Money, regulate the Value thereof, and of foreign Coin, and fix the Standard of Weights and Measures;

To provide for the Punishment of counterfeiting the Securities and current Coin of the United States;

To establish Post Offices and post Roads;

To promote the Progress of Science and useful Arts, by securing for limited Times to Authors and Inventors the exclusive Right to their respective Writings and Discoveries;

To constitute Tribunals inferior to the supreme Court;

To define and punish Piracies and Felonies committed on the high Seas, and Offenses against the Law of Nations;

To declare War, grant Letters of Marque and Reprisal, and make Rules concerning Captures on Land and Water;

To raise and support Armies, but no Appropriation of Money to that Use shall be for a longer Term than two Years;

To provide and maintain a Navy;

To make Rules for the Government and Regulation of the land and naval Forces;

To provide for calling forth the Militia to execute the Laws of the Union, suppress Insurrections and repel Invasions;

To provide for organizing, arming, and disciplining, the Militia, and for governing such Part of them as may be employed in the Service of the United States, reserving to the States respectively, the Appointment of the Officers, and the Authority of training the Militia according to the discipline prescribed by Congress;

To exercise exclusive Legislation in all Cases whatsoever, over such District (not exceeding ten Miles square) as may, by Cession of particular States, and the Acceptance of Congress, become the Seat of the Government of the United States, and to exercise like Authority over all Places purchased by the Consent of the Legislature of the State in which the Same shall be, for the Erection of Forts, Magazines, Arsenals, dock-Yards and other needful Buildings; -And

To make all Laws which shall be necessary and proper for carrying into Execution the foregoing Powers, and all other Powers vested by this Constitution in the Government of the United States, or in any Department or Officer thereof.

SECTION. 9

The Migration or Importation of such Persons as any of the States now existing shall think proper to admit, shall not be prohibited by the Congress prior to the Year one thousand eight hundred and eight, but a Tax or duty may be imposed on such Importation, not exceeding ten dollars for each Person

The Privilege of the Writ of Habeas Corpus shall not be suspended, unless when in Cases of Rebellion or Invasion the public Safety may require it.

No Bill of Attainder or ex post facto Law shall be passed.

[No Capitation, or other direct, Tax shall be laid, unless in Proportion to the Census or Enumeration herein before directed to be taken.]*

No Tax or Duty shall be laid on Articles exported from any State

No Preference shall be given by any Regulation of Commerce or Revenue to the Ports of one State over those of another: nor shall Vessels bound to, or from, one State, be obliged to enter, clear, or pay Duties in another.

No Money shall be drawn from the Treasury, but in Consequence of Appropriations made by Law; and a regular Statement and Account of the Receipts and Expenditures of all public Money shall be published from time to time.

No Title of Nobility shall be granted by the United States: And no Person holding any Office of Profit or Trust under them, shall, without the Consent of the Congress, accept of any present, Emolument, Office, or Title, of any kind whatever, from any King, Prince, or foreign State.

SECTION. 10

No State shall enter into any Treaty, Alliance, or Confederation; grant Letters of Marque and Reprisal; coin Money; emit Bills of Credit; make any Thing but gold and silver Coin a Tender in Payment of Debts; pass any Bill of Attainder, ex post facto Law, or Law impairing the Obligation of Contracts, or grant any Title of Nobility.

No State shall, without the Consent of the Congress, lay any Imposts or Duties on Imports or Exports, except what may be absolutely necessary for executing it's inspection Laws: and the net Produce of all Duties and Imposts, laid by any State on Imports or Exports, shall be for the Use of the Treasury of the United States; and all such Laws shall be subject to the Revision and Controul of the Congress.

No State shall, without the Consent of Congress, lay any Duty of Tonnage, keep Troops, or Ships of War in time of Peace, enter into any Agreement or Compact with another State, or with a foreign Power, or engage in War, unless actually invaded, or in such imminent Danger as will not admit of delay.

Article.   II.

SECTION. 1

The executive Power shall be vested in a President of the United States of America. He shall hold his Office during the Term of four Years, and, together with the Vice President, chosen for the same Term, be elected, as follows:

Each State shall appoint, in such Manner as the Legislature thereof may direct, a Number of Electors, equal to the whole Number of Senators and Representatives to which the State may be entitled in the Congress: but no Senator or Representative, or Person holding an Office of Trust or Profit under the United States, shall be appointed an Elector.

[The Electors shall meet in their respective States, and vote by Ballot for two Persons, of whom one at least shall not be an Inhabitant of the same State with themselves. And they shall make a List of all the Persons voted for, and of the Number of Votes for each; which List they shall sign and certify, and transmit sealed to the Seat of the Government of the United States, directed to the President of the Senate. The President of the Senate shall, in the Presence of the Senate and House of Representatives, open all the Certificates, and the Votes shall then be counted. The Person having the greatest Number of Votes shall be the President, if such Number be a Majority of the whole Number of Electors appointed; and if there be more than one who have such Majority, and have an equal Number of Votes, then the House of Representatives shall immediately chuse by Ballot one of them for President; and if no Person have a Majority, then from the five highest on the List the said House shall in like Manner chuse the President. But in chusing the President, the Votes shall be taken by States, the Representation from each State having one Vote; A quorum for this Purpose shall consist of a Member or Members from two thirds of the States, and a Majority of all the States shall be necessary to a Choice. In every Case, after the Choice of the President, the Person having the greatest Number of Votes of the Electors shall be the Vice President. But if there should remain two or more who have equal Votes, the Senate shall chuse from them by Ballot the Vice President.]*

The Congress may determine the Time of chusing the Electors, and the Day on which they shall give their Votes; which Day shall be the same throughout the United States.

No Person except a natural born Citizen, or a Citizen of the United States, at the time of the Adoption of this Constitution, shall be eligible to the Office of President; neither shall any person be eligible to that Office who shall not have attained to the Age of thirty five Years, and been fourteen Years a Resident within the United States

 In Case of the Removal of the President from Office, or of his Death, Resignation, or Inability to discharge the Powers and Duties of the said Office, the Same shall devolve on the Vice President, and the Congress may by Law provide for the Case of Removal, Death, Resignation or Inability, both of the President and Vice President, declaring what Officer shall then act as President, and such Officer shall act accordingly, until the Disability be removed, or a President shall be elected.]*

The President shall, at stated Times, receive for his Services, a Compensation, which shall neither be increased nor diminished during the Period for which he shall have been elected, and he shall not receive within that Period any other Emolument from the United States, or any of them.

Before he enter on the Execution of his Office, he shall take the following Oath or Affirmation:- "I do solemnly swear (or affirm) that I will faithfully execute the Office of President of the United States, and will to the best of my Ability, preserve, protect and defend the Constitution of the United States."

SECTION. 2

The President shall be Commander in Chief of the Army and Navy of the United States, and of the Militia of the several States, when called into the actual Service of the United States; he may require the Opinion, in writing, of the principal Officer in each of the executive Departments, upon any Subject relating to the Duties of their respective Offices, and he shall have Power to grant Reprieves and Pardons for Offenses against the United States, except in Cases of Impeachment.

He shall have Power, by and with the Advice and Consent of the Senate, to make Treaties, provided two thirds of the Senators present concur; and he shall nominate, and by and with the Advice and Consent of the Senate, shall appoint Ambassadors, other public Ministers and Consuls, Judges of the supreme Court, and all other Officers of the United States, whose Appointments are not herein otherwise provided for, and which shall be established by Law: but the Congress may by Law vest the Appointment of such inferior Officers, as they think proper, in the President alone, in the Courts of Law, or in the Heads of Departments.

The President shall have Power to fill up all Vacancies that may happen during the Recess of the Senate, by granting Commissions which shall expire at the End of their next Session

SECTION. 3

He shall from time to time give to the Congress Information of the State of the Union, and recommend to their Consideration such Measures as he shall judge necessary and expedient; he may, on extraordinary Occasions, convene both Houses, or either of them, and in Case of Disagreement between them, with Respect to the Time of Adjournment, he may adjourn them to such Time as he shall think proper; he shall receive Ambassadors and other public Ministers; he shall take Care that the Laws be faithfully executed, and shall Commission all the Officers of the United States

SECTION. 4

The President, Vice President and all civil Officers of the United States, shall be removed from Office on Impeachment for, and Conviction of, Treason, Bribery, or other high Crimes and Misdemeanors.

Article. III.

SECTION. 1

The judicial Power of the United States, shall be vested in one supreme Court, and in such inferior Courts as the Congress may from time to time ordain and establish. The Judges, both of the supreme and inferior Courts, shall hold their Offices during good Behaviour, and shall at stated Times, receive for their Services, a Compensation, which shall not be diminished during their Continuance in Office.

SECTION. 2

The judicial Power shall extend to all Cases, in Law and Equity, arising under this Constitution, the Laws of the United States, and Treaties made, or which shall be made, under their Authority; - to all Cases affecting Ambassadors, other public Ministers and Consuls; - to all Cases of admiralty and maritime Jurisdiction; - to Controversies to which the United States shall be a Party; - to Controversies between two or more States; - [between a State and Citizens of another State;-]* between Citizens of different States, - between Citizens of the same State claiming Lands under Grants of different States, [and between a State, or the Citizens thereof;- and foreign States, Citizens or Subjects.]*

In all Cases affecting Ambassadors, other public Ministers and Consuls, and those in which a State shall be Party, the supreme Court shall have original Jurisdiction. In all the other Cases before mentioned, the supreme Court shall have appellate Jurisdiction, both as to Law and Fact, with such Exceptions, and under such Regulations as the Congress shall make.

The Trial of all Crimes, except in Cases of Impeachment; shall be by Jury; and such Trial shall be held in the State where the said Crimes shall have been committed; but when not committed within any State, the Trial shall be at such Place or Places as the Congress may by Law have directed.

SECTION. 3

Treason against the United States, shall consist only in levying War against them, or in adhering to their Enemies, giving them Aid and Comfort. No Person shall be convicted of Treason unless on the Testimony of two Witnesses to the same overt Act, or on Confession in open Court.

The Congress shall have Power to declare the Punishment of Treason, but no Attainder of Treason shall work Corruption of Blood, or Forfeiture except during the Life of the Person attainted

Article. IV.

SECTION. 1

Full Faith and Credit shall be given in each State to the public Acts, Records, and judicial Proceedings of every other State. And the Congress may by general Laws prescribe the Manner in which such Acts, Records and Proceedings shall be proved, and the Effect thereof.

SECTION. 2

The Citizens of each State shall be entitled to all Privileges and Immunities of Citizens in the several States
A Person charged in any State with Treason, Felony, or other Crime, who shall flee from Justice, and be found in another State, shall on Demand of the executive Authority of the State from which he fled, be delivered up, to be removed to the State having Jurisdiction of the Crime.

 No Person held to Service or Labour in one State, under the Laws thereof, escaping into another, shall, in Consequence of any Law or Regulation therein, be discharged from such Service or Labour, but shall be delivered up on Claim of the Party to whom such Service or Labour may be due.]*

SECTION. 3

New States may be admitted by the Congress into this Union; but no new State shall be formed or erected within the Jurisdiction of any other State; nor any State be formed by the Junction of two or more States, or Parts of States, without the Consent of the Legislatures of the States concerned as well as of the Congress.

The Congress shall have Power to dispose of and make all needful Rules and Regulations respecting the Territory or other Property belonging to the United States; and nothing in this Constitution shall be so construed as to Prejudice any Claims of the United States, or of any particular State.

SECTION. 4

The United States shall guarantee to every State in this Union a Republican Form of Government, and shall protect each of them against Invasion; and on Application of the Legislature, or of the Executive (when the Legislature cannot be convened) against domestic Violence.

Article. V.

The Congress, whenever two thirds of both Houses shall deem it necessary, shall propose Amendments to this Constitution, or, on the Application of the Legislatures of two thirds of the several States, shall call a Convention for proposing Amendments, which in either Case, shall be valid to all Intents and Purposes, as Part of this Constitution, when ratified by the Legislatures of three-fourths of the several States, or by Conventions in three fourths thereof, as the one or the other Mode of Ratification may be proposed by the Congress; Provided that no Amendment which may be made prior to the Year One thousand eight hundred and eight shall in any Manner affect the first and fourth Clauses in the Ninth Section of the first Article; and that no State, without its Consent, shall be deprived of its equal Suffrage in the Senate

Article. VI.

All Debts contracted and Engagements entered into, before the Adoption of this Constitution, shall be as valid against the United States under this Constitution, as under the Confederation

This Constitution, and the Laws of the United States which shall be made in Pursuance thereof; and all Treaties made, or which shall be made, under the Authority of the United States, shall be the supreme Law of the Land; and the Judges in every State shall be bound thereby, any Thing in the Constitution or Laws of any State to the Contrary notwithstanding.

The Senators and Representatives before mentioned, and the Members of the several State Legislatures, and all executive and judicial Officers, both of the United States and of the several States, shall be bound by Oath or Affirmation, to support this Constitution; but no religious Test shall ever be required as a Qualification to any Office or public Trust under the United States

Article. VII.

The Ratification of the Conventions of nine States, shall be sufficient for the Establishment of this Constitution between the States so ratifying the Same.

Done in Convention by the Unanimous Consent of the States present the Seventeenth Day of September in the Year of our Lord one thousand seven hundred and Eighty seven and of the Independence of the United States of America the Twelfth In Witness whereof We have hereunto subscribed our Names,

Go. Washington--Presidt:
and deputy from Virginia

NEW HAMPSHIRE

John Langdon
Nicholas Gilman

MASSACHUSETTS

Nathaniel Gorham
Rufus King

CONNECTICUT

Wm. Saml. Johnson
Roger Sherman

NEW YORK

Alexander Hamilton

NEW JERSEY

Wil: Livingston
David Brearley
Wm. Paterson
Jona: Dayton

PENNSYLVANIA

B Franklin
Thomas Mifflin
Robt Morris
Geo. Clymer
Thos. FitzSimons
Jared Ingersoll
James Wilson
Gouv Morris

DELAWARE

    Geo: Read
    Gunning Bedford jun
    John Dickinson
    Richard Bassett
    Jaco: Broom

MARYLAND

    James McHenry
    Dan of St. Thos. Jenifer
    Danl Carroll

VIRGINIA

    John Blair-
    James Madison Jr.

NORTH CAROLINA

    Wm. Blount
    Richd. Dobbs Spaight
    Hu Williamson

SOUTH CAROLINA

    J. Rutledge
    Charles Cotesworth Pinckney
    Charles Pinckney
    Pierce Butler

GEORGIA

    William Few
    Abr Baldwin

Attest William Jackson Secretary

In Convention Monday
September 17th, 1787.
Present
The States of
New Hampshire, Massachusetts, Connecticut, Mr. Hamilton from New York, New Jersey, Pennsylvania, Delaware, Maryland, Virginia, North Carolina, South Carolina and Georgia.

Resolved,

That the preceeding Constitution be laid before the United States in Congress assembled, and that it is the Opinion of this Convention, that it should afterwards be submitted to a Convention of Delegates, chosen in each State by the People thereof, under the Recommendation of its Legislature, for their Assent and Ratification; and that each Convention assenting to, and ratifying the Same, should give Notice thereof to the United States in Congress assembled. Resolved, That it is the Opinion of this Convention, that as soon as the Conventions of nine States shall have ratified this Constitution, the United States in Congress assembled should fix a Day on which Electors should be appointed by the States which shall have ratified the same, and a Day on which the Electors should assemble to vote for the President, and the Time and Place for commencing Proceedings under this Constitution

That after such Publication the Electors should be appointed, and the Senators and Representatives elected: That the Electors should meet on the Day fixed for the Election of the President, and should transmit their Votes certified, signed, sealed and directed, as the Constitution requires, to the Secretary of the United States in Congress assembled, that the Senators and Representatives should convene at the Time and Place assigned; that the Senators should appoint a President of the Senate, for the sole Purpose of receiving, opening and counting the Votes for President; and, that after he shall be chosen, the Congress, together with the President, should, without Delay, proceed to execute this Constitution

By the unanimous Order of the Convention

Go. Washington-Presidt:
W. JACKSON Secretary.

* Language in brackets has been changed by amendment.

THE AMENDMENTS TO THE CONSTITUTION OF THE UNITED STATES AS RATIFIED BY THE STATES

Preamble to the Bill of Rights

Congress of the United States
begun and held at the City of New-York, on
Wednesday the fourth of March,

THE Conventions of a number of the States, having at the time of their adopting the Constitution, expressed a desire, in order to prevent misconstruction or abuse of its powers, that further declaratory and restrictive clauses should be added: And as extending the ground of public confidence in the Government, will best ensure the beneficent ends of its institution

RESOLVED by the Senate and House of Representatives of the United States of America, in Congress assembled, two thirds of both Houses concurring, that the following Articles be proposed to the Legislatures of the several States, as amendments to the Constitution of the United States, all, or any of which Articles, when ratified by three fourths of the said Legislatures, to be valid to all intents and purposes, as part of the said Constitution; viz.

ARTICLES in addition to, and Amendment of the Constitution of the United States of America, proposed by Congress, and ratified by the Legislatures of the several States, pursuant to the fifth Article of the original Constitution.

(Note: The first 10 amendments to the Constitution were ratified December 15, 1791, and form what is known as the "Bill of Rights.")

Amendment I.

Congress shall make no law respecting an establishment of religion, or prohibiting the free exercise thereof; or abridging the freedom of speech, or of the press, or the right of the people peaceably to assemble, and to petition the Government for a redress of grievances.

Amendment II.

A well regulated Militia, being necessary to the security of a free State, the right of the people to keep and bear Arms, shall not be infringed.

Amendment III.

No Soldier shall, in time of peace be quartered in any house, without the consent of the Owner, nor in time of war, but in a manner to be prescribed by law.

Amendment IV.

The right of the people to be secure in their persons, houses, papers, and effects, against unreasonable searches and seizures, shall not be violated, and no Warrants shall issue, but upon probable cause, supported by Oath or affirmation, and particularly describing the place to be searched, and the persons or things to be seized.

Amendment V.

No person shall be held to answer for a capital, or otherwise infamous crime, unless on a presentment or indictment of a Grand Jury, except in cases arising in the land or naval forces, or in the Militia, when in actual service in time of War or public danger; nor shall any person be subject for the same offence to be twice put in jeopardy of life or limb; nor shall be compelled in any criminal case to be a witness against himself, nor be deprived of life, liberty, or property, without due process of law; nor shall private property be taken for public use, without just compensation.

Amendment VI.

In all criminal prosecutions, the accused shall enjoy the right to a speedy and public trial, by an impartial jury of the State and district wherein the crime shall have been committed, which district shall have been previously ascertained by law, and to be informed of the nature and cause of the accusation; to be confronted with the witnesses against him; to have compulsory process for obtaining witnesses in his favor, and to have the Assistance of Counsel for his defence.

Amendment VII.

In suits at common law, where the value in controversy shall exceed twenty dollars, the right of trial by jury shall be preserved, and no fact tried by a jury shall be otherwise re-examined in any Court of the United States, than according to the rules of the common law.

Amendment VIII.

Excessive bail shall not be required, nor excessive fines imposed, nor cruel and unusual punishments inflicted.

Amendment IX.

The enumeration in the Constitution, of certain rights, shall not be construed to deny or disparage others retained by the people.

Amendment X.

The powers not delegated to the United States by the Constitution, nor prohibited by it to the States, are reserved to the States respectively, or to the people.

AMENDMENTS 11-27

Amendment XI.

Passed by Congress March 4, 1794. Ratified February 7, 1795.

(Note: A portion of Article III, Section 2 of the Constitution was modified by the 11th Amendment.)

The Judicial power of the United States shall not be construed to extend to any suit in law or equity, commenced or prosecuted against one of the United States by Citizens of another State, or by Citizens or Subjects of any Foreign State.

Amendment XII.

Passed by Congress December 9, 1803. Ratified June 15, 1804.

(Note: A portion of Article II, Section 1 of the Constitution was changed by the 12th Amendment.)

The Electors shall meet in their respective states, and vote by ballot for President and Vice-President, one of whom, at least, shall not be an inhabitant of the same state with themselves; they shall name in their ballots the person voted for as President, and in distinct ballots the person voted for as Vice-President, and they shall make distinct lists of all persons voted for as President, and of all persons voted for as Vice-President, and of the number of votes for each, which lists they shall sign and certify, and transmit sealed to the seat of the government of the United States, directed to the President of the Senate;-the President of the Senate shall, in the presence of the Senate and House of Representatives, open all the certificates and the votes shall then be counted;-The person having the greatest number of votes for President, shall be the President, if such number be a majority of the whole number of Electors appointed; and if no person have such majority, then from the persons having the highest numbers not exceeding three on the list of those voted for as President, the House of Representatives shall choose immediately, by ballot, the President. But in choosing the President, the votes shall be taken by states, the representation from each state having one vote; a quorum for this purpose shall consist of a member or members from two-thirds of the states, and a majority of all the states shall be necessary to a choice. [And if the House of Representatives shall not choose a President whenever the right of choice shall devolve upon them, before the fourth day of March next following, then the Vice-President shall act as President, as in case of the death or other constitutional disability of the President.-]* The person having the greatest number of votes as Vice-President, shall be the Vice-President, if such number be a majority of the whole number of Electors appointed, and if no person have a majority, then from the two highest numbers on the list, the Senate shall choose the Vice-President; a quorum for the purpose shall consist of two-thirds of the whole number of Senators, and a majority of the whole number shall be necessary to a choice. But no person constitutionally ineligible to the office of President shall be eligible to that of Vice-President of the United States.

*Superseded by Section 3 of the 20th Amendment.

Amendment XIII.

Passed by Congress January 31, 1865. Ratified December 6, 1865.

(Note: A portion of Article IV, Section 2 of the Constitution was changed by the 13th Amendment.)

SECTION 1

Neither slavery nor involuntary servitude, except as a punishment for crime whereof the party shall have been duly convicted, shall exist within the United States, or any place subject to their jurisdiction.

SECTION 2

Congress shall have power to enforce this article by appropriate legislation.

Amendment XIV.

Passed by Congress June 13, 1866. Ratified July 9, 1868.

(Note: Article I, Section 2 of the Constitution was modified by Section 2 of the 14th Amendment.)

SECTION 1

All persons born or naturalized in the United States and subject to the jurisdiction thereof, are citizens of the United States and of the State wherein they reside. No State shall make or enforce any law which shall abridge the privileges or immunities of citizens of the United States; nor shall any State deprive any person of life, liberty, or property, without due process of law; nor deny to any person within its jurisdiction the equal protection of the laws.

SECTION 2

Representatives shall be apportioned among the several States according to their respective numbers, counting the whole number of persons in each State, excluding Indians not taxed. But when the right to vote at any election for the choice of electors for President and Vice President of the United States, Representatives in Congress, the Executive and Judicial officers of a State, or the members of the Legislature thereof, is denied to any of the male inhabitants of such State, [being twenty-one years of age,]* and citizens of the United States, or in any way abridged, except for participation in rebellion, or other crime, the basis of representation therein shall be reduced in the proportion which the number of such male citizens shall bear to the whole number of male citizens twenty-one years of age in such State.

SECTION 3

No person shall be a Senator or Representative in Congress, or elector of President and Vice President, or hold any office, civil or military, under the United States, or under any State, who, having previously taken an oath, as a member of Congress, or as an officer of the United States, or as a member of any State legislature, or as an executive or judicial officer of any State, to support the Constitution of the United States, shall have engaged in insurrection or rebellion against the same, or given aid or comfort to the enemies thereof. But Congress may by a vote of two-thirds of each House, remove such disability.

SECTION 4

The validity of the public debt of the United States, authorized by law, including debts incurred for payment of pensions and bounties for services in suppressing insurrection or rebellion, shall not be questioned. But neither the United States nor any State shall assume or pay any debt or obligation incurred in aid of insurrection or rebellion against the United States, or any claim for the loss or emancipation of any slave; but all such debts, obligations and claims shall be held illegal and void.

SECTION 5

The Congress shall have the power to enforce, by appropriate legislation, the provisions of this article.

*Changed by Section 1 of the 26th Amendment.

Amendment XV.

Passed by Congress February 26, 1869. Ratified February 3, 1870.

SECTION 1

The right of citizens of the United States to vote shall not be denied or abridged by the United States or by any State on account of race, color, or previous condition of servitude.

SECTION 2

The Congress shall have the power to enforce this article by appropriate legislation.

Amendment XVI.

Passed by Congress July 2, 1909. Ratified February 3, 1913.

(Note: Article I, Section 9 of the Constitution was modified by the 16 ʰ Amendment.)

The Congress shall have power to lay and collect taxes on incomes, from whatever source derived, without apportionment among the several States, and without regard to any census or enumeration.

Amendment XVII.

Passed by Congress May 13, 1912. Ratified April 8, 1913.

(Note: Article I, Section 3 of the Constitution was modified by the 17th Amendment.)

The Senate of the United States shall be composed of two Senators from each State, elected by the people thereof, for six years; and each Senator shall have one vote. The electors in each State shall have the qualifications requisite for electors of the most numerous branch of the State legislatures.

When vacancies happen in the representation of any State in the Senate, the executive authority of such State shall issue writs of election to fill such vacancies: Provided, That the legislature of any State may empower the executive thereof to make temporary appointments until the people fill the vacancies by election as the legislature may direct.

This amendment shall not be so construed as to affect the election or term of any Senator chosen before it becomes valid as part of the Constitution.

Amendment XVIII.

Passed by Congress December 18, 1917. Ratified January 16, 1919. Repealed by the 21 Amendment, December 5, 1933.

SECTION 1

After one year from the ratification of this article the manufacture, sale, or transportation of intoxicating liquors within, the importation thereof into, or the exportation thereof from the United States and all territory subject to the jurisdiction thereof for beverage purposes is hereby prohibited.

SECTION 2

The Congress and the several States shall have concurrent power to enforce this article by appropriate legislation.

SECTION 3

This article shall be inoperative unless it shall have been ratified as an amendment to the Constitution by the legislatures of the several States, as provided in the Constitution, within seven years from the date of the submission hereof to the States by the Congress.

Amendment XIX.

Passed by Congress June 4, 1919. Ratified August 18, 1920.

The right of citizens of the United States to vote shall not be denied or abridged by the United States or by any State on account of sex.

Congress shall have power to enforce this article by appropriate legislation.

Amendment XX.

Passed by Congress March 2, 1932. Ratified January 23, 1933.

(Note: Article I, Section 4 of the Constitution was modified by Section 2 of this Amendment. In addition, a portion of the 12th Amendment was superseded by Section 3.)

SECTION 1

The terms of the President and the Vice President shall end at noon on the 20th day of January, and the terms of Senators and Representatives at noon on the 3d day of January, of the years in which such terms would have ended if this article had not been ratified; and the terms of their successors shall then begin.

SECTION 2

The Congress shall assemble at least once in every year, and such meeting shall begin at noon on the 3d day of January, unless they shall by law appoint a different day.

SECTION 3

If, at the time fixed for the beginning of the term of the President, the President elect shall have died, the Vice President elect shall become President. If a President shall not have been chosen before the time fixed for the beginning of his term, or if the President elect shall have failed to qualify, then the Vice President elect shall act as President until a President shall have qualified; and the Congress may by law provide for the case wherein neither a President elect nor a Vice President shall have qualified, declaring who shall then act as President, or the manner in which one who is to act shall be selected, and such person shall act accordingly until a President or Vice President shall have qualified.

SECTION 4

The Congress may by law provide for the case of the death of any of the persons from whom the House of Representatives may choose a President whenever the right of choice shall have devolved upon them, and for the case of the death of any of the persons from whom the Senate may choose a Vice President whenever the right of choice shall have devolved upon them.

SECTION 5

Sections 1 and 2 shall take effect on the 15th day of October following the ratification of this article.

SECTION 6

This article shall be inoperative unless it shall have been ratified as an amendment to the Constitution by the legislatures of three-fourths of the several States within seven years from the date of its submission.

Amendment XXI.

Passed by Congress February 20, 1933. Ratified December 5, 933.

SECTION 1

The eighteenth article of amendment to the Constitution of the United States is hereby repealed.

SECTION 2

The transportation or importation into any State, Territory, or possession of the United States for delivery or use therein of intoxicating liquors, in violation of the laws thereof, is hereby prohibited.

SECTION 3

This article shall be inoperative unless it shall have been ratified as an amendment to the Constitution by conventions in the several States, as provided in the Constitution, within seven years from the date of the submission hereof to the States by the Congress.

Amendment XXII.

Passed by Congress March 21, 1947. Ratified February 27, 951.

SECTION 1

No person shall be elected to the office of the President more than twice, and no person who has held the office of President, or acted as President, for more than two years of a term to which some other person was elected President shall be elected to the office of President more than once. But this Article shall not apply to any person holding the office of President when this Article was proposed by Congress, and shall not prevent any person who may be holding the office of President, or acting as President, during the term within which this Article becomes operative from holding the office of President or acting as President during the remainder of such term.

SECTION 2

This article shall be inoperative unless it shall have been ratified as an amendment to the Constitution by the legislatures of three-fourths of the several States within seven years from the date of its submission to the States by the Congress.

Amendment XXIII.

Passed by Congress June 16, 1960. Ratified March 29, 1961.

SECTION 1

The District constituting the seat of Government of the United States shall appoint in such manner as Congress may direct:

A number of electors of President and Vice President equal to the whole number of Senators and Representatives in Congress to which the District would be entitled if it were a State, but in no event more than the least populous State; they shall be in addition to those appointed by the States, but they shall be considered, for the purposes of the election of President and Vice President, to be electors appointed by a State; and they shall meet in the District and perform such duties as provided by the twelfth article of amendment.

SECTION 2

The Congress shall have power to enforce this article by appropriate legislation.

Amendment XXIV.

Passed by Congress August 27, 1962. Ratified January 23, 1964.

SECTION 1

The right of citizens of the United States to vote in any primary or other election for President or Vice President, for electors for President or Vice President, or for Senator or Representative in Congress, shall not be denied or abridged by the United States or any State by reason of failure to pay poll tax or other tax.

SECTION 2

The Congress shall have power to enforce this article by appropriate legislation.

Amendment XXV.

Passed by Congress July 6, 1965. Ratified February 10, 1967.
(Note: Article II, Section 1 of the Constitution was modified by the 25th Amendment.)

SECTION 1

In case of the removal of the President from office or of his death or resignation, the Vice President shall become President.

SECTION 2

Whenever there is a vacancy in the office of the Vice President, the President shall nominate a Vice President who shall take office upon confirmation by a majority vote of both Houses of Congress.

SECTION 3

Whenever the President transmits to the President pro tempore of the Senate and the Speaker of the House of Representatives his written declaration that he is unable to discharge the powers and duties of his office, and until he transmits to them a written declaration to the contrary, such powers and duties shall be discharged by the Vice President as Acting President.

SECTION 4

Whenever the Vice President and a majority of either the principal officers of the executive departments or of such other body as Congress may by law provide, transmit to the President pro tempore of the Senate and the Speaker of the House of Representatives their written declaration that the President is unable to discharge the powers and duties of his office, the Vice President shall immediately assume the powers and duties of the office as Acting President.

Thereafter, when the President transmits to the President pro tempore of the Senate and the Speaker of the House of Representatives his written declaration that no inability exists, he shall resume the powers and duties of his office unless the Vice President and a majority of either the principal officers of the executive department or of such other body as Congress may by law provide, transmit within four days to the President pro tempore of the Senate and the Speaker of the House of Representatives their written declaration that the President is unable to discharge the powers and duties of his office. Thereupon Congress shall decide the issue, assembling within forty-eight hours for that purpose if not in session. If the Congress, within twenty-one days after receipt of the latter written declaration, or, if Congress is not in session, within twenty-one days after Congress is required to assemble, determines by two-thirds vote of both Houses that the President is unable to discharge the powers and duties of his office, the Vice President shall continue to discharge the same as Acting President; otherwise, the President shall resume the powers and duties of his office.

Amendment XXVI.

Passed by Congress March 23, 1971. Ratified July 1, 1971.

(Note: Amendment 14, Section 2 of the Constitution was modified by Section 1 of the 26th Amendment.)

SECTION 1

The right of citizens of the United States, who are eighteen years of age or older, to vote shall not be denied or abridged by the United States or by any State on account of age.

SECTION 2

The Congress shall have power to enforce this article by appropriate legislation.

Amendment XXVII.

Originally proposed Sept. 25, 1789. Ratified May 7, 1992.

No law, varying the compensation for the services of the Senators and Representatives, shall take effect, until an election of representatives shall have intervened.

Source: The National Constitution Center (NCC), www.constitutioncenter.org

Index

References are given by chapter and section number (e.g., 5.3 = Chapter 5, Section 3). Abbreviations used: Prol. = Prologue; Intro = Introduction; SB = Sidebar; Epil. = Epilogue; App. = Appendix.

A

AARP, 5.4
Act of Congress (Kaiser), App. B
Administrative Assistant, 2.5
Advise and Consent, 2.3 (SB)
Advocacy advertising, 4.9
Advocacy organizations, 5.3
Advocate's Pledge, App. C
Al Franken, Giant of the Senate (Franken), App. B
All Politics Is Local (O'Neill and Hymel), App. B
Alzheimer's Association, 5.8 (SB)
Amber Alert system, 5.2
Amending legislation, 2.4, 2.6, App. A
American flags, requests for, 2.5
Anthrax attack, 7.0
Appropriations, 2.3, 2.6 (SB), 6.2, App. A
Aspin, Les, 4.3
Authorization, legislation, App. A

B

Baker, Russell, 7.5
Baucus, Max, 2.3
Beckmann, David, 7.6 (SB)
Biden, Joe, 5.2 (SB)
Bill, App. A. *See also* Legislation
Bipartisan Policy Center, 5.3 (SB)
Birnbaum, Jeffrey H., 4.5
Bismarck, Otto von, 2.4
Boston Marathon Bombing, 5.2 (SB)
Boston Tea Party, 5.9
Brandeis, Louis, 2.4
Budget
    discretionary spending, App. A
    for congressional offices, 1.3
    federal apportionment of, 4.10
    nondiscretionary spending, App. A
    resolution, App. A
Burke, Edmund, Prol.
Burns, Ken, Prol.
Bush, George W., 7.6 (SB)

C

C-SPAN, 2.6, 7.4
Cialdini, Robert B., 6.0
Campaign contributors' influence on legislative decision-making, 4.7
Campaign finance laws, 4.7
Carnegie, Dale, 5.3
Casework, 1.2
Caseworker/Field Representative, 2.5
Casey, Bob, 4.1
Center for Effective Lawmaking, 5.3 (SB)
Chairman's mark, 2.4, 2.6, App. A
Checks and balances, Prol., 3.0
Chief of Staff, 2.5
Children as letter writers, 1.5
Churchill, Winston, 7.0
Chylinski, Manya, 5.2 (SB)
Civil Rights era, 5.9
Clinton, Bill, 4.9
Clinton, Hillary, 4.1
Cloture, App. A
Club for Growth, 5.3
Cole, Tom, 2.3
Colleagues influencing legislative decision-making, 4.3
Committees
    assignments, 6.2
    chairmen, 2.4
    conference, App. A, App. D
    hearings, 2.4, 2.6, App. A

influencing committee staff, 5.6
role of, 2.4
report language, 2.6, App. A
Communications Director, 2.5
Community Project Funding, 6.2. *See also*
Earmarks
Congress at a Crossroads (Sobol and
Steinhorn), App. B
Congress Overwhelmed (LaPira, Drutman,
and Kosar), App. B
Congressional Accountability Act, 2.1
Congressional Budget Office (CBO), App. A
Congressional culture, 2.0–2.6
committees, 2.4
power hierarchy, 2.2
staff hierarchy, 2.5
working environment, 2.1
work schedule, 1.4
Congressional Deskbook (Koempel and
Schneider), App. A
Congressional Management Foundation,
1.4, 2.3 (SB), 3.2, 3.3, 4.5, 5.3 (SB), 5.4,
6.3, 6.6 (SB), 6.7, 6.9, 7.4
Congressional offices, 1.0–1.7
answering mail, 1.5, 1.6
budget, 1.3
casework, 1.2
committee offices, 2.4
constituents' dominant role, 1.1
legislative work of (Washington
office), 1.2
representational work of (district or
state office), 1.2
small business analogy, 1.3
staffing, 2.5
types of, 1.2
Congressional Research Service (CRS),
App. A
Constituents' dominant role, 1.1
Constituents' influence on decision-
making, 2.3, 5.4
Constitution, U.S., App. E
Continuing resolution, App. A
Correspondence. *See* Mail and email
COVID-19 pandemic, 6.3
Culture. See Congressional culture

D

Daley-Harris, Sam, App. B
Davis, Danny, 2.5
Dear Colleague Letters, 2.6, App. A
Dear Mr. Congressman (Lowell), 7.1
Decision-making by legislators, 3.0–3.3.
See also Influences on legislative
decision-making
policy research and
conscience and, 3.1
data and, 3.2
influences on, 5.4
Defense, Department of, 2.2
Democratic Caucus, App. A
Digital Director, 2.5, 7.4
Dirksen, Everett, 2.6
Discharge petition, App. A
District Director, 2.5
Drutman, Lee, App. B

E

Earmarks, 2.3, 2.6 (SB), 6.2, App. A. *See
also* Community Project Funding
Esterling, Kevin, 6.6 (SB)
Economic and political footprint, 5.5
Editorial, newspaper, 5.4
Eilperin, Juliet, 2.3 (SB)
Email. *See* Mail and email
Environmental Protection Agency (EPA),
1.5, 2.6
Events, set up, 5.10, 6.9
Expertise
of lobbyists, 4.6
of constituents, 4.6
of staff, 2.5

F

Facebook, 2.5, 2.6, 7.4
Family influence on legislative decision-
making, 4.1
Federal agencies, resolving problems with,
1.2
Federal Emergency Management Agency
(FEMA), 5.2 (SB)

Feedback to lobbyists, 6.2
Fenno, Richard, Prol., App. B
Field Representative, 2.5
Filibuster, 2.2, App. A
FMC (The Association of Former Members of Congress), App. B
Foley, Thomas, 2.3 (SB)
Follow-up after meetings, 6.2
Frank, Barney, 2.0, 4.7, App. B
Franken, Al, App. B
Freshman legislators, 5.10

G

Gingrich, Newt, 2.6
Giffords, Gabby, 5.9, 6.4
Government Accountability Office (GAO), 2.6
GovTrack, 5.3 (SB)
Granger, Kay, 2.3
Grassroots organizing and advocacy, 4.6, 5.5 (SB)

H

Haley's Act, 5.2
Hamilton, Lee, Prol.
Handouts for meetings, 6.5
Harry and Louise ads on health care reform, 4.9
Harvard University, 6.6 (SB)
Health care reform, 1.7, 4.9
Hearings, 2.4, 2.6, App. A
Heather's Law, 5.2
Heikkila, Larry, 2.3
Hollywood, 2.3 (SB)
Home Style (Fenno), Prol., App. B
House
        committees, 2.4
        duties legislative, 1.2
        duties representational, 1.2
        rules, 2.2, App. A
        Rules Committee, 2.2, App. A
        institutional character, 2.2
        size of districts, 2.2
        staff role of, 2.5, 6.7
        types of work performed, 1.2

Human Rights Campaign, 5.3
Humphrey, Hubert H., 7.5
Hunger relief, 7.5
Hymel, Gary, App. B

I

Influences on legislative decision-making
        campaign contributors, 4.7
        colleagues, 4.3
        constituents, 5.4
        editorial, newspaper, 5.4
        email and mail, 5.4
        friends and families, 4.1
        knowledgeable acquaintances, 4.2
        leadership pressure, 4.4
        letter to the editor, 5.4
        lobbyists, 4.5
        meetings, 5.4
        paid advertising, 4.9
        phone calls, 5.4
        polling, 4.8
        social media, 5.4
        town hall meetings, 5.4
"I'm Just a Bill," 2.6, 5.2 (SB)
Interns, 2.5
Iran-Contra hearings, Prol., 2.4

J

Jefferson, Thomas, Prol., 2.2
Johnson, Mike, 2.2

K

Kaiser, Robert, App. B
Kilmer, Derek, 2.6 (SB)
Kennedy, Edward M., 6.7
Kennedy, John F., 6.7
Knowledgeable acquaintances as influences on legislative decision-making, 4.2
Koempel, Michael L., App. A, App. D
Kohl, Herb, 2.3 (SB)
Kosar, Kevin R., App. B

L

LaPira, Timothy M., App. B
Lame duck session, App. A
Lazer, David M.J., 6.6 (SB)
Leadership pressure on legislator decision-making, 4.4
League of Conservation Voters (LCV), 5.3
Legis1, 5.3 (SB)
Legislation
    committee process of producing, 2.4
      App. D
    legislator's knowledge of bill
      contents, 3.3
    markup process, 2.4
    voice votes, 2.4
    voting up or down on amendments,
      2.4
Legislative Assistant (LA), 1.2, 2.5, 6.7
Legislative Correspondent (LC), 2.5
Legislative Counsel, 2.5
Legislative Director (LD), 2.5
Legislative office
    calling, 7.2
    Washington office, 1.2, 2.1
    working environment for staff, 2.1
Letters to the editor, 7.3
Lincoln, Abraham, Prol., Epil.
Lobbyists, Intro., 4.5, 4.6, 5.4, 6.2
Long-term relationships and influence on
    legislative decision-making, 5.3
Lowell, Juliet, 7.1
Luciano, Jennifer, 2.5
Lugar Center, 5.3 (SB)
Lugar, Richard, 5.3 (SB), 7.6 (SB)

M

Madison, James, Prol., 3.0, App. E
Mail and email
    campaign with action alert, 1.6, 4.6,
      5.4
    children as writers, 1.5
    effectiveness of, 1.5, 1.6, 7.1, 5.4
    how to write effectively, 3.2, 7.1
    number of, to get attention, 4.5
    passion for cause, 1.5

    representing a group, 1.5
    responding to, 1.6
    Systems Administrator's role, 2.5
    thank you notes, 1.5, 6.7, 7.7
Markup process, 2.4, 2.6, App. A
McCarthy, Joe, 2.4
McCarthy, Kevin, 2.2, 4.4
Mead, Margaret, Epil.
Media, local, 7.5
*Media Relations Handbook for Government,
    Associations, Nonprofits, and Elected
    Officials* (Fitch), 6.9
Meetings
    chance meetings, 6.1 (SB)
    duration of, 6.2
    early arrival, 6.2
    follow-up, 6.2, 6.9
    in-state, 6.4, 5.10
    influencing staff, 6.5, 6.7
    presentation for, 6.2
    research prior to, 5.3
    scheduling, 6.1
    size of, 6.2
    specificity of request, 6.2
    telephone town hall meetings, 6.6
    tips for, 6.2
    town hall meetings, 6.5
    value of, 5.4
    virtual, 6.3, 5.4
Megan's Law, 5.2
Millennium Challenge Account, 7.6 (SB)
Moore, Barry, 6.4
Murrow, Edward R., Intro.

N

National Alzheimer's Project Act (NAPA),
    5.8 (SB)
National Court Reporters Association
    (NCRA), 5.4
National Education Association (NEA), 5.4
National Rifle Association (NRA), 5.3, 5.4
Neblo, Michael A., 6.6 (SB)
New Hampshire House of Representatives,
    6.1
9/11, 1.5
Nonprofit organizations, affiliation and
    influence of, 5.4

Notes, of congratulations, 5.10
Nussle, Jim, 2.6

O

O'Neill, Tip, 2.6, App. B
Office Manager, 2.5
Offices. *See* Congressional offices
Ohio State University, 6.6 (SB)
Omnibus bill, App. A
One-minute speech, 2.6, App. A
Oversight hearings, 2.4

P

Paid advertising's influence on legislative
    decision-making, 4.9
Personal offices of congress, 1.1–1.6, 2.1,
    2.5
Personal stories as influential in legislative
    decision-making, 3.2, 5.2
at town hall meetings, 6.5
Petitions to Congress, 7.6
Phone banks to advocate cause, 7.2
Phone calls to legislators, 5.4, 7.2
Police, U.S. Capitol, 5.9
Political Action Committee, 5.4
Politics with the People (Neblo, Esterling,
    Lazer), 6.6 (SB)
Polling, 4.8
Portman, Rob, 2.2
Post-Disaster Mental Health Response Act,
    5.2 (SB)
Press release, 2.6
Pressley, Ayanna, 5.2 (SB)
Press Secretary/Communications Director,
    2.5

R

Rachel's Law, 5.2
Recess, App. A
Reclaiming Our Democracy (Daley-Harris),
    App. B
Reconciliation bill, App. A
Republican Conference, App. A
Representational work (district or state
    office), 1.2

Research work
    of congressional offices, 1.2
    use in legislator decisions, 3.2
    prior to face-to-face meetings, 5.3
Resources, list of Washington and
    Congress, 5.3 (SB)
Ripley, Amanda, 2.6 (SB)
Rider, to a bill, App. A
Rise Against Hunger, 7.5
Roberts, John, 6.2
Rosenblatt, Alan, 7.8
Rules, of the House, 2.2, App. A

S

Scalise, Steve, 5.9
Scheduler, 2.5
Schneider, Judy, App. A, App. D
Select Committee on the Modernization of
    Congress, 2.1, 2.6 (SB), App. B
Senate
    committees, 2.4
    duties legislative, 1.2
    duties representational, 1.2
    filibuster, 2.2
    institutional character, 2.2
    staff role of, 6.7
    types of work performed, 1.2
Senior Legislative Assistant, 2.5
Sherrington, Charles, 7.8
Sinema, Kyrsten, 2.2
Small business analogy, 1.3
Sobol, Mark, App. B
Social media, 2.6, 5.4, 5.10, 7.4
Sojourner Truth, 2.5
Special interests, power of, Intro., 4.5, 4.6,
    5.4
Speaker of the House, 2.2, 2.3 (SB)
Special Order, 2.6, App. A
Specificity of request, 6.2
Staff Assistant, 2.5
Staff of congressional offices
    hierarchy of staff, 2.5
    influencing staff, 6.7, 6.9
    job descriptions, 2.5
    office management and, 1.3
    working environment for, 2.1

Stark, Pete, 5.2
State Director, 2.5
Statistics, use of, 3.2
Steinhorn, Leonard, App. B
Subcommittee chairmen, 2.2, 2.4
Systems Administrator, 2.5

T

Tauberer, Joshua, 5.3 (SB)
Teachers unions, 5.4
Thank you notes, 1.5, 7.7
Threats, avoid making, 5.9
Timing for influencing legislative decision-making, 5.1
Timmons, William, 2.6 (SB)
Town hall meetings
    in-person, 5.4, 6.5
    telephone, 5.4, 6.6, 6.6 (SB)
    virtual, 6.6
Tribes on the Hill (Weatherford), 2.0
Trump, Donald, 5.9, 6.4, 6.5
Tuberville, Tommy, 2.2
Twain, Mark, 7.4
Twitter. *See* X

U

Udall, Mo, 5.1
University of California-Riverside, 6.6 (SB)

V

Veto, App. A, App. D
Vietnam War, 5.9
Voice votes, 2.4

W

Wallach, Philip A., Prol., App. B
War votes, 4.8
Washington, George, 2.2, App. E
Watergate hearings, 2.4
Weatherford, Jack McIver, 2.0
Wells Fargo Bank, Prol.
West Wing, 2.3 (SB)
Why Congress (Wallach), Prol., App. B
Wyden, Ron, 2.3
Wick, Connie, 7.6 (SB)
Wronsky, Suzanne, 5.8 (SB)
Working environment of congressional offices, 2.1
Work schedule, 1.4

X

X, 2.5, 2.6, 7.4

About the Author

Bradford Fitch is the former CEO of the Congressional Management Foundation (CMF). He has spent 40 years in Washington as a journalist, congressional aide, consultant, college instructor, internet entrepreneur, and writer/researcher. He is a leading trainer of citizen-advocates in the U.S., with more than 50,000 Americans having participated in one of his programs.

Fitch got his start in communications as a DJ for his local AM radio station in Upstate New York at the age of 16. He went on to become a radio and television reporter, and later spent 13 years on Capitol Hill, serving as a press secretary, legislative director, and chief of staff. From 2001–2005 he served as Deputy Director of CMF. He left in 2006 to form a new software company, Knowlegis, which is now part of FiscalNote. In 2010 he returned to CMF, where he served as CEO for 14 years.

Fitch is also the author of *Media Relations Handbook for Government, Associations, Nonprofits, and Elected Officials*. His work and interviews have appeared in *The New York Times*, *The Washington Post*, CBC News, and NPR, among other outlets. He also taught journalism and public communications at American University in Washington, D.C, where he served as an adjunct Associate Professor of Communications.

About Legis1

Legis1 is a next-generation legislative intelligence platform that leverages advanced AI and robust analytics to deliver unparalleled insight into the inner workings of Congress and the government affairs industry. Designed for professionals seeking to build connections, harness data-driven insights, and maximize impact, Legis1 transforms complex political data into actionable knowledge.

Legis1's intuitive interface is built around three core capabilities:

Data-Driven Insights:

- Leverage integrated data, advanced analytics, and AI tools to identify patterns, predict congressional activity, and assess the policy landscape around customizable issue areas
- Analyze member and committee communications and messaging trends using AI-enhanced analytics and keyword searches of more than 1 million communications from 1998-present
- Analyze member offices and committees by legislative effectiveness, voting record, staff compensation, turnover, and experience

Connection Building:

- Map influence through an expansive, interlinked network of Member of Congress, congressional staffers, witnesses, government affairs professionals, donors, and lobbyists
- Study the connections and capital flows between lobbyists, their clients, and Congress
- Access directories of staffers and lobbyists with profiles featuring issue areas and contact information (email, phone, address)

Research Efficiency:

- Access 20+ years of legislative history and congressional hearings, complete with AI-generated summaries and searchable transcripts
- Track every local and national news article mentioning Members of Congress, analyze media coverage by lawmaker and media outlet, and assess social media following and reach
- Explore 20+ years of congressional witness testimony and Member questions, complete with analytics and sentiment analysis

With Legis1, go beyond rhetoric and uncover the reality of political decision-making — driven by data, enhanced with AI, and grounded in facts.

Request a Demo

About The Sunwater Institute

The Sunwater Institute is a nonpartisan, nonprofit think tank dedicated to strengthening the foundations of liberal democracy through interdisciplinary science, technology, and open dialogue.

Guided by the belief that transparency, civic participation, and informed debate are essential to a thriving democracy, Sunwater brings together thought leaders and publishes research and practical resources that elevate public policy conversations. From demystifying the legislative process to equipping citizens with the tools to engage effectively, Sunwater helps individuals and institutions alike navigate and shape American governance today.

Explore More Sunwater Books

Sunwater publishes a growing collection of authoritative guides on lawmaking, advocacy, and civic engagement, including:

- *Testifying Before Congress* — A practical guide to assist witnesses and their organizations in preparing and delivering Congressional testimony
- *Congressional Procedure* — An insider's look at the formal and informal rules of lawmaking
- *Congressional Deskbook* — A comprehensive guide to Congress
- *The Legislative Drafter's Desk Reference* — Best practices for drafting clear, effective legislative language
- *Media Relations Handbook* — Guidance for public officials, advocates, and experts on communicating a message and working with the press

Learn more about Sunwater's full catalog of publications by scanning the QR code below.

Stay Informed

Scan the QR code below to sign up for Sunwater's newsletter and receive timely updates on new releases, expert commentary, and upcoming events.

www.ingramcontent.com/pod-product-compliance
Lightning Source LLC
Chambersburg PA
CBHW041933260326
41914CB00010B/1277